Ethics in Action for Cub Scouts

BOY SCOUTS OF AMERICA

Copyright 1991
Boy Scouts of America
Irving, Texas
ISBN 0-8395-3015-3
No. 3015
Printed in U.S.A.

Contents

5 Introduction
8 Reflecting
10 Helping
13–64 **Ethics in Action Activities**
- 14 Be A Friend
- 18 Be Aware and Care—1
- 21 Be Aware and Care—2
- 26 Caring and Sharing
- 29 Consumer Alert
- 31 Differences
- 34 Fire! Fire!
- 38 Hard Lessons
- 46 Kindness Counts
- 48 Peace Is . . .
- 51 Saying Hello, Saying Goodbye
- 53 Saying No!
- 57 Shoplifting Is Just Plain Wrong
- 60 What We Say

63 When Bad Things Happen

Introduction

What is Ethics in Action?

Ethics in Action is an activities program for Cub Scouts designed to reinforce the character-building goals that have always been a part of the program of the Boy Scouts of America. Ethics in Action activities encourage Cub Scouts and their leaders to "think a little deeper" about values and about some of the decisions and consequences of decisions that are a normal part of growing up. The activities also try to enhance boys' respect and concern for others by helping them see things from different points of view. But above all, Ethics in Action activities are fun. They are part of the **"game with a purpose"** that is Scouting.

The Ethics in Action Program

There are 14 activity modules in the Ethics in Action program. Each is built around a single theme. The themes are:

Be a Friend. Promotes discussion of what friendship means, and how friends act toward each other.

Be Aware and Care—1. Discusses physical handicaps with an emphasis on blindness.

Be Aware and Care—2. Discusses other physical handicaps, suggests ways to prepare for getting to know elderly people.

Caring and Sharing. A mock court scenario is used to deal with the issues of taking care of one's own things and showing respect for the property of others.

Consumer Alert. Helps boys analyze commercial messages on television and in printed advertisement.

Differences. Explores attitudes towards differences in people.

Fire! Fire! Explores the responsible use of fire and deals with the kinds of decisions regarding fire that Cub Scouts and Webelos Scouts are likely to face.

Hard Lessons. Shows boys what it is like to have learning disabilities and underscores the need for understanding problems faced by children and adults with learning disabilities.

Kindness Counts. Stresses responsibility to animals, both at home and in the wild.

Peace Is . . . Discusses ways to introduce the positive aspects of peace and suggests ways boys can contribute to worldwide understanding and peace.

Saying Hello, Saying Goodbye. Provides ways to help boys who are joining or leaving the group.

Saying No! Helps reinforce information that boys already know about personal safety, drug use, etc., through production of a public service announcement.

Shoplifting Is Just Plain Wrong. This activity involves a field trip to see a store security system and provides information that boys should know about the consequences of shoplifting.

What We Say. Deals with name-calling and tale-bearing that, though typical behavior for boys of this age, can be disruptive and painful.

A final section, **When Bad Things Happen,** provides help for leaders in discussing special problems of an individual Scout or of the group.

There are two parts to each Ethics in Action activity:

- A concrete experience shared by the group
- Reflecting, a guided discussion that helps boys "make sense" of the experience and explore the deeper meaning it contains

The parts are equally important. A videotape and the Reflecting section of this book explain more about how reflecting is done. The Helping section discusses ways in which service to others also encourages the development of values.

Why an Ethics in Action Program?

WHY TRY TO TEACH VALUES?

Today's Cub Scouts are growing up in a very complicated world. They are faced with conflicting messages that are often hard to sort out. Some influences—peer pressure, for example—may provide boys with the positive support they need to help them do the right thing. Or peer pressure may work the other way and urge boys to act in ways that sharply contradict the positive values that their parents are trying to encourage.

Since the very beginning, the program of the Boy Scouts of America has been an educational experience concerned with values. The first Scouting activities were designed back in 1907 to fill what the movement's founder, Lord Robert S. S. Baden-Powell called the "chinks" left by the education that boys received in school. One of these "chinks," according to Baden-Powell, was character. The others were physical fitness, practical skills, and service to others. All of these remain key parts of Cub Scouting today.

However, when parents in Minnesota's Viking Council were asked what more they wished Cub Scouting could do, they said they would like more help teaching their sons to make good decisions based on sound values. Nearly 80 years after the beginning of the Boy Scouts of America, parents still see character as a chink in their sons' formal education! As a result, the Viking Council and the Center for Youth Development and Research at the University of Minnesota, under the leadership of Dr. Judith B. Erickson, developed the Ethics in Action program.

Ethics in Action for Cub Scouts was created to answer parents' requests for help. Ethics in Action activities enhance character formation; that is, the development and reinforcement of the worthwhile qualities that are part of the Cub Scout Promise and Law of the Pack.

Ethics in Action activities are designed to build boys' ability to sort out values. They stress cooperation and open communication between adult Scouters and boys, and among the Cub Scouts themselves. The "reflecting" process provides opportunities to express real feelings without fear of a put-down or ridicule that is so much a part of the culture of American boys. Ethics in Action activities help Cub Scouts develop skills, as well as confidence in and respect for self and others. The program also helps boys understand that their actions may affect others, as well as themselves.

How Ethics in Action Works

Ethics in Action has been designed specifically for boys of Cub Scout age. The activities take into account typical age-related patterns of physical, mental, social, and moral growth during middle childhood. (Some of the changes that take place as boys grow are explained in the videotape, *Ages and Stages.*) In addition to being developmentally appropriate, Ethics in Action activities are challenging and relevant to youth. Ethics in Action experiences encourage growth through such processes as:

- Creating cognitive conflict in situations where things are not as they are thought to be, and by providing experiences that challenge preconceived ideas and prejudices

- Comparing different perspectives that help in learning to see things from someone else's viewpoint
- Providing action opportunities to try new things, gain new information or new skills, and express feelings
- Presenting problem-solving situations that will increase their sense of competence and empower them to make good decisions
- Introducing role models who will help them see better ways of dealing with situations that involve ethical decisions
- Giving opportunities for open, guided reflection so that they can "make sense" of their shared experiences and learn to express their true feelings

Using Ethics in Action

Each Ethics in Action activity is introduced in the same easy-to-follow format so that leaders may fit them into the regular den schedule. Many of the activities require little preparation, and all can be managed by first-time as well as experienced leaders. Councils will provide leader training to introduce and explain the new materials. Various activities will be discussed in greater detail at roundtables throughout the year.

Most of the activities have been designed for use in a typical den of five to eight boys. A few can be done in larger groups, but for "reflecting" session, boys should be divided into sections of no more than 8 boys.

Ethics in Action Format

Each set of Ethics in Action activities is presented in this format:

Overview. Explains the purpose of the activity and why it is important and provides some background information for the leader.

Preparation. Discusses appropriate activity sites, lists materials needed, and describes any other necessary advance planning.

Action. Describes how to conduct the activity. It includes suggestions for reflecting on the experience the boys have just had. Some of the modules also include ideas for follow-up activities, either at home or within the den at another time.

Resources. Lists of organizations or reference materials that relate to the activity.

When the activities require recording forms or other printed materials, master copies are included for the leader to reproduce so that each boy has one.

Cub Scout Involvement

Where possible, the Cub Scouts should help prepare for the activity. They can, for example, help in the choice of activity, field-trip site, or guest participants.

Safety

Safety must be a primary concern in using the Ethics in Action program. We have tried to anticipate and point out situations requiring special attention but, of course, others may arise. We urge that leaders review all den and pack safety procedures as part of the planning process.

Reflecting

Reflecting includes:

- thinking about a past experience, and
- expressing these thoughts out loud.

Ethics in Action activities are interesting and fun—but they all have deeper ideas behind them. Reflecting is the way that a leader can guide boys to their own understanding of the deeper purpose of the activity.

Ground Rules

Regardless of the number of boys who take part in an activity, the discussions should be carried out in small groups (no more than eight boys). The first thing for the group to do is to agree on some ground rules for the discussion. Reflecting should not be used as an opportunity for an argument about what happened, or who did what to whom. Neither should the leader consider it his or her chance to deliver a moral lecture. Rather, it is a chance for all who have shared an experience to think a little deeper about it and share their thoughts. The group members should be encouraged to develop their own rules for talking about and evaluating what took place. If they need some help in getting started, here are some suggestions that have worked well for other groups:

- Everyone (both leaders and boys) should respect and listen to everyone else. Everyone should reserve judgment.
- Everyone is encouraged to offer a point of view, as well as say how he feels about it
- No one has to talk if he doesn't feel like it.

The boys will undoubtedly come up with some other ground rules they wish to try out.

Questions

Most young boys have had only limited experiences to draw from in forming opinions. Therefore, they may need some guidance if they are to get to the deeper point that the activity is designed to make. The leader can guide their exploration, not by giving them adult answers or opinions, but by asking the kinds of questions that will help the boys discover those deeper meanings for themselves.

This kind of guided discussion is sometimes called *processing*. Processing, or reflecting, is the key to learning from experience. Guided reflection requires some thinking in advance on the part of the leader. As part of the planning for an Ethics in Action activity, the leader should think through what he or she wants the boys to get out of the experience. The leader should come prepared with some questions that will start to draw out the thoughts of the boys. Some ways to do this are:

Ask open-ended questions. Ask questions that cannot be answered with a simple yes or no, but require some explanation.

Ask feeling questions. Ask the boys to reflect on how they felt while they were doing the activity—and about how they feel now that it is over.

Ask judgment questions. Ask the boys to give opinions and to make decisions about things, even if those things are their feelings.

Ask guiding questions. Know where you want the discussion to go and steer a course that stays on track.

Use closing questions. Toward the end, get the boys to think about pulling their ideas together and drawing some conclusions as a group.

Every Ethics in Action activity should include time for discussion and reflection. Each set of activities includes a section on "reflecting." We have provided some basic ideas and raised some issues that we think are important. To get you started, there are examples of the types of questions we have described above. Each question is labelled with a letter standing for the type of question that it is (O = open-ended; F = feeling; J = judgment; G = guiding; and C = closing). Don't worry too much about the exact kinds of questions that get asked, as long as the discussion is moving and is stretching the boys' thinking. The specific content of every discussion will be unique—based on what actually took place and the "reflections" of the particular group of boys who were part of it.

Why We Do Reflecting

As we have already said, Ethics in Action activities are interesting and fun—but they have a deeper idea behind them. Scouting is a "game with a purpose." Ethics in Action activities try to help boys understand the values that are part of the Cub Scout Promise and the Law of the Pack, and connect them to their daily lives. These activities are designed to help them understand that they have the power to choose how they will act, and that the choices they make have consequences. Understanding such lessons does not come automatically. Values are learned by the "doing" of them.

The American educator John Dewey pointed out many years ago that every experience a child has is to some extent a moving educational force, because that experience can affect, for better or worse, the attitudes that will influence future experiences. But, Dewey also noted, not every experience is equally worthwhile. The value of an experience "can be judged only on the basis of what it moves toward and into." He went on to say that adults have a responsibility to act as judges and guides of the experiences offered to children, if they expect these experiences to open new paths of growth.

More recent research has shown the wisdom of Dewey's observations. Educators have compared values education programs that led to greater moral and social development and those that do not. The differences, it turned out, were not strongly related to the specific experiences the young people had. Rather, the researchers found, programs that worked included a period of guided reflection on what the experience was all about. Creating experiences and helping young people to reflect and form attitudes that will lead to growth are the heart of Ethics in Action.

Holding discussions with young boys is not always easy. Many of them have had few opportunities to express their deeper thoughts and feelings—particularly among peers. Boy culture generally, with its emphasis on competition and put-downs, does not encourage risking such expression. But the experiences that leaders have had with Ethics in Action activities encourages us to believe that good discussion is possible, if you keep trying! The *Reflecting* videotape shows how it can be done.

It is reflecting and processing that help youngsters make sense of experiences. They are asked to use their skills of observation, and to add up facts and feelings in a new way. It is here that learning takes place. Learning *how to learn from experience* gives them power to influence the way events affect them. They learn that what they do, or do not do, can make a difference. It is this sense of power within themselves that will help them resist pressures that come from outside. And it is the knowledge that they have some power to control the meaning of events that leads them toward greater self-respect and sensitivity to others.

Helping

Helping means a lot of things:

- Doing your share so that jobs get done easier or faster or so the burden doesn't fall on one or just a few people
- Doing part of someone else's work
- Doing something for the benefit of someone in need

Any way you look at it, helping means *doing*. Helping is truly Ethics in Action. Several of the activities include ideas for useful follow-up service projects. You will discover that these projects involve being with and helping people, not "doing things," like cleaning up the environment or "making things" like tray favors (although these can also be important and useful). When Cub Scouts and Webelos Scouts follow up their Ethics in Action activity with a project that helps other people, they:

- fulfill the Cub Scout Promise to "do their best . . . to help other people," and they get reinforcement for the idea that ethical "thinking" also means "doing"
- make a connection between "doing the right thing" in their den activities and "doing the right thing" in the world around them
- become real resources — that is, useful citizens — for their communities

There is general agreement that good youth service programs have certain characteristics, including:

- activities that are genuinely useful, and get young people directly involved with the people they are helping
- activities that are challenging, yet appropriate for the developmental levels of the young people who are helping
- a strong introduction at the place where the young people will be helping, that includes a clear explanation about what needs to be done and how the youths will do it
- good supervision while they are helping, from caring, well-informed adults
- time for reflection — that is, a chance to blend experience and thought so as to "make sense" out of it and add to the positive impact of what they have experienced

When young people take part in well-planned programs that help people, there are some predictable outcomes. One of the most important is that some real needs of people in the community are met. Beyond the effects on others, however, helping others has some effects on the young people themselves. They:

- learn to assume responsibility and to cooperate better with each other in getting things done
- increase their problem-solving skills
- develop more understanding of social problems and more positive attitudes to people in need of help
- develop an increased sense of competence and power as well as self-esteem

It appears that giving service to others can help to build the character and self-confidence of young people.

The idea that we should help others is our inheritance from past generations. We must keep this idea alive so that it can become our legacy to pass on to future generations.

Youth Service Through the Years

When Baden-Powell placed service to others at the heart of the Scouting program, he saw doing a daily Good Turn as a bridge to good citizenship. He felt that helping others was another way that the movement could fill one of the "chinks" in boys' education. In stressing service, he was building on a solid inheritance from youth organizations of the past.

The first organized groups for American children began to appear nearly 100 years before Boy Scouting came to America in 1910. From the very beginning, helping others was an important part of their programs. In those early days, for example, butter and sugar were real luxuries and many young church group members gave them up. Then these young people asked their parents for the money that had been saved so that they could give it to the poor or send it to the missions. In the 1830s, thousands of children belonged to the Cold Water Army (an organization very much like today's Just Say No! clubs). They collected food, clothing, and firewood for poor families.

Especially in times of war, children were called upon to do their parts. During the Civil War, for example, the Alerts sewed uniforms for Union soldiers and made bandages for the wounded. During World War I, a group called the Go-Hawks supported Belgian war orphans with the money they earned from the sale of tin-foil they collected. Of course, by this time, there were Boy Scouts, Girl Scouts, Camp Fire Girls, and 4-H Clubs. They helped raise hundreds of thousands of dollars for the war bond drives, planted and tended acres of "victory gardens," knitted thousands of socks and afghan squares, and even collected tons of nut shells that were made into gas mask filters. After the fighting was over, the Junior Red Cross made rooms full of sturdy furniture and collected mountains of books that they sent to schools all over Europe to replace things destroyed in the war.

So, when Cub Scouts and Webelos Scouts promise "to help other people," they are taking part in the rich tradition of youth service that they have inherited from generations of American children past. When they put their promise into practice, they keep that heritage alive for generations yet to come.

Youth Service Today

Americans have begun to realize that a grown-up "me generation" is having some profound effects on our cherished institutions. The 1980s saw families, governments, religious organizations, businesses, banks, the military, and educational institutions rocked by a succession of scandals originating in personal ambition.

Many believe that these scandals that involve prominent people are making today's young people cynical and suspicious. Concerned adults fear that youths are becoming "disconnected" from the traditional civic values that have held our nation together. They see evidence of the isolation of young people in the U.S. rates of teen parenthood, suicide, and alcohol and drug abuse, which are the highest in the Western world. They argue that the balance between being concerned with individual rights and being concerned with responsibilities to others has been badly upset. There is a growing interest in youth service programs as a way of correcting this imbalance.

Across the nation, in many settings and in many ways, young people from kindergarten to their early 20s are being encouraged to become active resources for their communities. The growth of the youth service movement is leading to more research about what makes a good program, and about the effects that service programs can have on young participants and on their communities. The ideas that we have used in the Ethics in Action program are based on this research.

The suggestions for service that are part of Ethics in Action for Cub Scouts are just a beginning, to help you get started. There are many other things that you can do. For example, some of the ideas for helping people in *Cub Scout Program Helps* will fit right in with the activities. You and the boys will be able to think of many other ways to help people you know in your own community.

Ethics in Action activities can make a difference. One leader reported that for years, Christmas caroling at a local nursing home had been a pack activity, but only a few boys had shown up to do it. After going through the Be Aware and Care—2 activities that helped the boys understand some of the problems elderly people have, they had 100 percent participation from the pack!

I don't know what your destiny will be, but the one thing I know; the only ones among you who will really be happy are those who will have sought and found how to serve.

Albert Schweitzer

Everybody can be great because everybody can serve.

Martin Luther King, Jr.

We become just by performing just acts.

Aristotle

Ethics in Action Activities

Be A Friend

These activities promote discussion of what friendship means and how friends act toward one another.

Overview

Children need friends! They need friends to do things with, to talk to, and just to be with. Yet, not all children are as skillful at making friends as we might like them to be. Research shows that youngsters who do not have friends in the early grade-school years—the Cub Scout years—are more likely to have social adjustment and mental health problems later in life.

Cub Scouting comes at an important time in boys' lives. Between about the ages of 6 and 8, they will begin to understand that other people have points of views also. They also begin to understand and take into account the motives of others, in explaining behavior. They are learning to do what social psychologists call "taking the role," or seeing the viewpoint of other people. At first, they can do this only for one person at a time. This period corresponds to explanations of moral choices based on expectation of punishment or reward.

By about age 8 to 10, youngsters start to understand that not only can person A understand the viewpoint of person B, but person B will also be able to understand the viewpoint of person A. Young people begin to see the give and take of relationships. This ability to see a situation from another person's point of view corresponds to seeing solutions to moral dilemmas in terms of "you scratch my back, and I'll scratch yours."

As children approach early adolescence (at the age of about 10 to 12), they begin to be able to step back from situations, and see them from a more generalized perspective. Although at any age they may act in ways that are kind and generous, it is only at the point when they can generalize that they are able to understand and discuss the full meaning of the "golden rule."

It is important for the formation of friendships that children learn how to adjust their actions to the expectations of others in appropriate ways. The standards that youngsters use to control behavior in their peer groups will be related to the mental and moral development that is typical for their age groups. A boy too much out of step with other boys of his age may experience problems in making and keeping friends. Boys without friends still have needs for acceptance, and they can become vulnerable to negative peer pressure. Cub Scouting should be a place where positive friendships between and among boys and adults can form and grow. It should be a place where some of the hard lessons of "getting along," as well as the easy ones, can be learned with the support of friends.

"Be a Friend" is designed to guide youngsters to thinking about what friendship means.

Preparation

Activity site: This activity requires a space large enough to allow all the boys' drawings to be spread on the floor, with enough work area to complete them without getting in each other's way.

Materials:

- **Sheets of inexpensive roll paper** cut into pieces about a foot longer than the boys are tall. Newspaper offices often sell the left-over ends of newsprint rolls at low cost. These work well, but any sheet of paper wide and long enough is suitable.
- **Dark-colored crayons or chalk** (something that will write easily on the paper, but not stain clothing) to draw the basic outline.

Action

Each Cub Scout lies down in the middle of his sheet of paper, while an adult leader carefully traces the outline of his body. Boys are then "paired up" to continue the activity.

The boy should draw in his eyes, nose, and mouth, and indicate the outlines of clothing, so that he can identify the drawing as a picture of himself. (Coloring in the larger areas may take too much time at a meeting and can be done at home.)

REFLECTING

As the boy finishes the drawing, he and his partner begin to talk about what a friend should do and not do. Choose one side of the drawing for a "What Friends Do" list, and the other for a "What Friends Don't Do" list. Using the guiding questions, they might start talking about ways that eyes can be used to help friendship (watch out for danger, like a car coming) or hurt friendship (look at someone else's paper at school). Starting with the head, they might continue in this way until they get down to the feet, which can help (go bike riding with you) or hurt (kick you), and so on.

The Cub Scouts may want to compare their lists. The discussion might be built around such questions as:

- How does it feel when someone smiles at you? How does it feel when someone makes a face or sticks out his tongue at you? **(F)**
- What was your favorite part of this activity? **(C)**

Followup

Cub Scouts might take home the drawings of themselves and fasten them to their closet doors. They can then add to their lists of the "Do's" and "Don'ts" of friendship as they think of new things. They can look at their posters each morning as reminders of things to do to be good friends that day.

New kids in school frequently have a hard time making new friends. Through this activity, Cub Scouts can make newcomers feel welcome.

Note: Boys of Cub Scout and Webelos Scout age are beginning to be very conscious of the way they look. When this activity was tried out with older boys, they were asked to pair up and draw each other's outlines. Their efforts tended to be somewhat "crude," quickly prompting outcries of "You made me look weird on purpose!" The arguments that followed totally defeated the purpose of the activity. We suggest that even with older boys, it would be better to have a den chief or adult do the outline drawing. A long waiting time for getting everyone's drawing done is not good either. If there are not enough "outliners" available to do them all in a fairly short time, adaptations are needed.

Some possibilities:

1. Have each Scout draw a picture of his best friend, then go on to list what makes that person a good friend, or
2. Have each Scout draw a picture of himself. Choose one side for the "Friends Do" side, and the other for the "Friends Don't Do" side. Make lists, and use the drawings to stimulate discussion as suggested above.
3. Have each Scout draw two pictures: one of his best friend and one of himself. Make a "Friends Do" and "Friends Don't Do" list to go with each drawing. Are the lists with each drawing the same? If they are different, why?

The "Do's and Don'ts" drawing on the next page may be duplicated and substituted for a drawing done by the boys themselves.

DOs and DON'Ts

Look at the stick figure and think about how people use their bodies to be friends with others. How do they use their mouths, ears, hands, and so on? What should friends avoid doing?

Fill in your ideas on the lines below.

FRIENDS DO: FRIENDS DON'T:

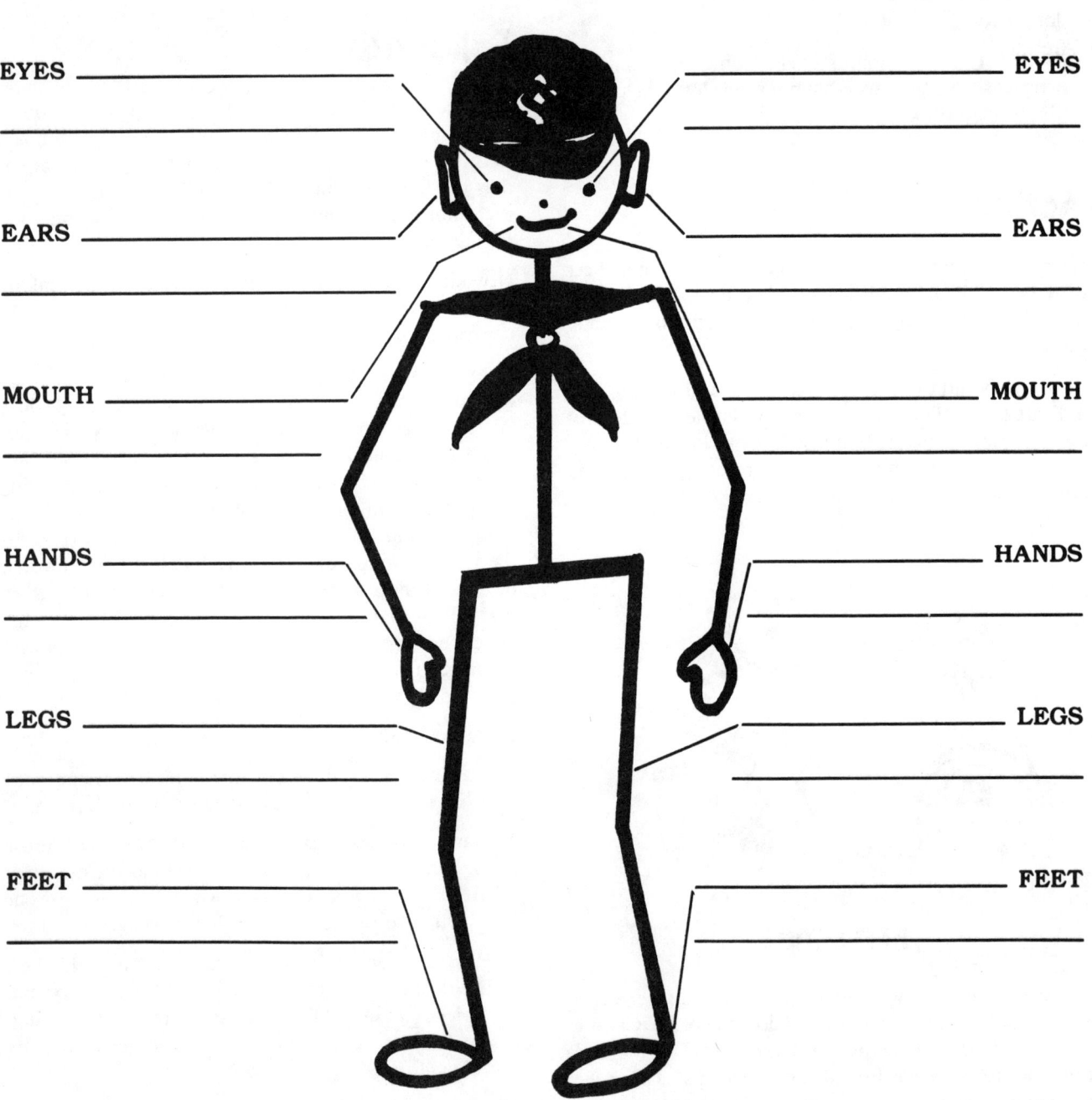

EYES _____ EYES

EARS _____ EARS

MOUTH _____ MOUTH

HANDS _____ HANDS

LEGS _____ LEGS

FEET _____ FEET

Reflecting Questions

- How can you let someone know you would like to be friends? **(O)**
- Do you have any friends who are more than a couple of years older or younger than you? What makes these friends special? **(O)**
- What do you think of first when you close your eyes and remember a good friend? **(G)**
- How does it feel if a friend ignores you? How does it feel when a friend lets you down? **(F)**
- Are there different kinds of friends? **(C)**

Be Aware and Care—1

This game is used as a springboard for discussing handicaps. The emphasis of the game is on blindness.

Overview

Until a few years ago, children with disabling handicaps rarely attended school in regular classrooms. They either were sent to special schools or segregated in separate units. This is no longer true of most public school systems. Physically challenged youngsters are now mainstreamed and do all or part of their schoolwork in regular classrooms. Mainstreaming emphasizes two principles:

- The need for handicapped youth to make their way in a world where most people do not share their special needs

- The need for nonhandicapped persons to know and understand people with needs different from their own

Given that 10 to 15 percent of all children have some form of handicap, it is safe to assume that most boys of Cub Scout age will know another child with special needs. He may be one of the boys in the pack.

Children of this age can be very supportive; they can also be very cruel. The 8- to 9-year-old is just beginning to be conscious of his appearance, and tends to do a lot of measuring of himself against his peers. Children with a strong sense of self should have no need to "put down" others who do not "measure up" to themselves. However, even basically kind children can get caught up in teasing others, especially when it is started as a group action by peers they admire.

Most schools where mainstreaming is practiced have introduced "handicap awareness" programs as part of the curriculum. The Cub Scout den or pack can reinforce attitudes of understanding. Children with special needs should be welcomed to Cub Scouting; any needs for modifications in activities should be worked out in advance with their parents. Leaders may wish to refer to the BSA publication, *Understanding Cub Scouts with Handicaps,* No. 3839A, that discusses these issues.

Lost in Space

This game is designed to sensitize boys to the problems of blindness or very limited vision. As with many of the activities, it includes reflective discussion, where the Cub Scouts are encouraged to express their reactions and feelings. This activity works well with 8- to 10-year-olds. Two to three dens (up to about 25 Cub Scouts) can do it together.

Preparation

Activity site: This activity requires a large area free from hazards such as stumps or access to streets. (If done indoors, a gym-sized room is suitable.) There should be several adults present to stand at the fringes of the playing area and keep the blindfolded boys within it.

Materials: An effective blindfold for every boy in the group except one.

Action

Explain to the boys that they are going to be "lost in space." Perhaps something has gone wrong with their space station and all of the lights have gone out. They cannot see it, but they must find it if they are to be safe. One boy is chosen to be the space station. He is the only one without a blindfold. All of the others must find the space station without being able to see it.

The boys should be spread out around the playing area and their blindfolds tied so that they cannot see or make out the shape of the space station. When all are blindfolded, tell them to turn around three times before starting their search. In the meantime, the "Space Station" is moved to a new location, where he remains for the rest of the game.

Being unable to see, the boys will have to rely on hearing. They all start to move toward what they hope is the space station. Each time someone bumps into another searcher, he must say, "beep beep." The person he bumps must answer "beep beep" also. When a boy finds the real space station, his "beep beep" signal is not answered. Rather, the "space station" silently takes his hand, and he knows that he is "home," and safe. Keeping very quiet, the searcher then removes his blindfold, and he becomes part of the "space station." This action continues until all are "safe."

Reflecting Questions

After the first round of play, have all sit down in groups of six to eight to discuss what happened. (Larger groups do not work well.) Some of the points that should be raised can be made with the folowing questions (if they don't come up naturally):

- Did you feel a little worried (although not necessarily actually afraid) when you were not able to see? **(F)**

- How did you figure out where the "space station" was? By listening closely for just a single "beep beep" signal? **(F)**

Typically, many of them will have tried to "peek." You might ask:

- Could a person who was completely blind peek? **(G)**

They can be reminded that there is no possibility of peeking for a person who is totally blind.

Once they have expressed their reactions to having to try to find something without being able to see it, you may want to ask:

- How does a person who cannot see well know where to go? **(G)**

Discuss some of the ways people cope with that, such as using a guide dog or using a cane that warns a person of something in the way and, when tapped, gives clues by the sounds it makes.

The boys should also understand that people who are blind or have very limited vision are by no means helpless. They very quickly get used to places and, once things are familiar, they get around well. However, whenever anything is moved from its usual place, the person with limited vision should be told about the change. Some people who don't see well may need help in new places until they get used to where things are.

Some other questions you might ask:

- How could we be of help to people who cannot see when they are in a new place, or when things have been moved around? **(O)**

- If you meet a person with a white cane who seems to need help in finding an address, what could you do? **(O)**

Some groups have gone on to discuss other handicaps. You might start them thinking with a question like:

- Are there times when a person who can see might feel like you did when you first played this game? **(O)**

One den decided that coming to the United States from another country and not knowing English might resemble a handicap like blindness or deafness, because you wouldn't understand what was going on around you.

Most groups will want to play the game more than once. Games should be ended before the group tires. Two times, at the most three, are enough for this one.

VARIATION

This is an adaptation of a New Games Foundation game called "Prui." Other variations can be invented. For example, instead of being "lost in space," they might take a theme from Kipling's *Jungle Book* and be lost in a very dark jungle. They must find Baloo, the wise old bear, to be safe from harm. As they bump into each other while blindfolded, they ask, "Baloo?" and are answered "Baloo!" by all but the "bear," who is silent and takes the hand of the person as the space station does in Lost in Space.

Followup

Invite a person who has impaired vision to attend a den meeting. Ask your guest to discuss his or her life, and to explain how to know when to offer help to a person who does not see well.

When one den found it impossible to get together with a blind boy, they made up a list of questions they wanted to ask him. Their leader (who was this boy's teacher) interviewed him and recorded his answers. Den members listened to the tape at another meeting. (Of course, the leader had asked both the boy and his parents for permission to do this.)

Learn how guide dogs are trained and how they should be treated by strangers.

There are many exciting new devices being developed to help people with poor vision get around. Find out about some of them, and how they help.

Be Aware and Care—2

These activities allow Cub Scouts to experience handicaps such as deafness, poor vision, difficulty in moving around freely, speech problems, and memory loss. The activities are a way of preparing boys for visits to elderly residents at nursing homes.

Overview

Boys of Cub Scout age likely have good basic health, good vision, hearing, taste, smell, and touch. Most will also have good basic physical coordination. All in all, most boys will be well equipped to take on what life has to offer. About 10 to 15 percent of American school children, however, have physical disabilities or chronic illnesses that are severe enough to limit their activities. A much higher proportion of elderly people will have disabilities or poor health.

Peers: It is often hard for the young and healthy to imagine not being that way. Because boys of this age are becoming very conscious of their own bodies, they are eager to make comparisons. They can be very cruel to peers who do not reach their own childish standards. For boys of Cub Scout age, standards are based on what they, themselves, are able to do. Mainstreaming has brought many physically challenged and chronically ill youngsters into regular classrooms. They need sensitive and understanding friends.

The Elderly: Young boys can also be very inconsiderate of the elderly—that is, if they think about them at all. Many will live too far away to make regular visits to grandparents and older relatives. Furthermore, far more of the elders whom they do know will be active and in relatively good health. However, as modern medicine has allowed people to live longer, the population of oldest Americans is growing more rapidly than any other age category. Most older people still live in their own homes, and wish to continue to do so for as long as they are able. With a little help, this time can be extended by several years. Some neighborhoods and communities have developed programs that enable youth to offer assistance to older residents.

Many younger American families are choosing to have their older relatives come to live with them. Some of the Cub Scouts may have grandparents living with their families. If invited, these grandparents could well become good friends of the whole den. They might also be valuable resources willing to share information and skills.

Actually, only about 5 percent of the nation's elderly live in nursing homes at any given time. Yet this is the group that we hear the most about. It remains true that many nursing home residents have no families, or are cut off from family members by distance (or, in some cases, poor relationships). Most nursing homes welcome visits from Cub Scouts (with planning in advance, of course). Such an event conducted by a pack or den may be a youngster's first contact with the very old and frail. Some of the boys will be quite unprepared for their meeting, and possibly even afraid. Many nursing homes encourage long-term friendships between their residents and young people. These relationships often turn out to be a source of growth and enrichment for both. Such friendships can do much to ease children's fears of aging.

Preparation

The activities below may be used to increase general awareness of disabilities, and the limitations that such physical challenges may place on peers. The emphasis, however, is on simulation of common losses experienced by many people as they grow older. They can be used as preparation for any venture that brings Cub Scouts and elderly people together.

There are many different parts to this activity. It is better to make choices and have time for discussion than to try to do them all.

Discussion: The activities should begin with a conversation about growing older and the natural changes that take place. Encourage the boys to share experiences they have had already. (It might help leaders to remember that to a Cub Scout, anyone past 30 may seem absolutely ancient and that they may need some help getting things into perspective.) Some of the things to bring up are the ways that these normal changes may make daily living more difficult and, also, that many people who have problems find it hard to admit that they can no longer do things that once were easy for them. Aging requires many adjustments, and by experiencing the effects of some of the disabilities associated with aging, Cub Scouts can gain insight and understanding of ways that they can help. They may need reminding that not every elderly person has all of these difficulties.

Action

Remember: There are a lot of choices in this set of activities. Don't try to do too much in one meeting. We have included some reflecting questions in each section.

Hearing

Materials: Cotton balls for each boy; one radio.

1. The leader *carefully* places cotton balls in the ears of all but one of the boys. The one without the cotton balls will be the observer. Have the boys carry on a group conversation in a normal tone of voice. Have the observer also speak in a normal tone and record what he sees and hears going on in the group.

   - Did people seem to hear what was being said? Were certain voices harder to hear? Did the boys with the cotton in their ears actually speak louder than they normally would? (This almost always happens.) **(O)**

2. Sometimes hearing is made more difficult because a person has a constant ringing or buzzing in the ears. Choose a boy who does not have cotton in his ears to be the observer. Have him turn on the radio to a level that is comfortable for him. Have the rest of the group begin several conversations at once (as might happen at a family gathering, for example). The observer then counts all of the "What's," "Whadyasay's," "Huhs," etc. that he hears.

   In discussing this experience, have the boys try to imagine what it would be like having to deal with constant background noise.!

   - Do they think this would make them talk more, or less? **(O)**

   - How did they feel when they could not hear some of what was being said? Would they want to carry on conversations when they were part of large noisy groups? **(F)**

3. Have the boys choose partners. After one has had a try, reverse roles. Have one boy with cotton balls in his ears further deaden the sound by placing his hands firmly over his ears. His partner then mouths a conversation, making no sound, moving only his lips. The "deaf" partner tries to understand by reading his lips. (You may want to write out some action words such as "fire," "explosion," "surprise," etc., for them to read to their partners, and then have them move on to three-word phrases.)

   - How much was understood? Were certain words easier to pick out? Did the speaking partner make more than usual use of his hands or facial expressions to try to get his message across? Did these gestures help? **(O)**

Discussion: When the Cub Scouts are reflecting on their experiences, there should be some guiding questions to help them remember that not all elderly people have hearing problems, and that many who do are helped by medications or hearing aids.

Followup

Ask the boys to watch a half-hour television program (with parental permission) with the sound turned off. Could they understand the program by the action only? Could they lip-read some of the conversations? What were their feelings when they could not follow the story? What aids are available for people with impaired hearing? What are trained "hearing dogs" and how do they help?

Learn how the deaf communicate by signing with their hands, lip-reading, or vocalizing. (See how to give the Cub Scout Promise and Law of the Pack in American Sign Language in *Scouting for the Hearing Impaired,* No.3061.)

Vision

Older people frequently experience changes in vision. Some of the common problems are nearsightedness (that is, they can't see things far away), farsightedness (that is, they can't see things up close), cataracts (a clouding-over of the lens of the eye), loss of peripheral vision, tunnel vision, and complete blindness.

Materials: Hand lotion; large squares of paper; several old pairs of glasses. (If these cannot be accumulated from the boys' families, many opticians have some that they will be willing to loan. If you explain the types of problems you are trying to simulate, they will probably be willing to mark the glasses for you and explain why the lenses correct the problem.)

1. Have the boys sit quietly and look through the various pairs of glasses.

    - How does the world look through the glasses? What is different? **(O)**

    Have youngsters or adults who wear glasses tell the group about what they can see with and without them. Talk about how important it is for everyone to protect their eyes and how critical glasses can be for people who wear them. Also explain that not all vision problems can be corrected with glasses. Some people cannot see well, even with glasses.

2. To simulate cataracts, start with a pair of glasses that have a slight correction. Smear hand lotion over the outer surface of the lenses and look through them.

    - How much can they see? How clear is it? **(O)**
    - What problems might a person with cataracts have? What adaptations might they have to make in their lives? **(G)**

    Explain that cataracts are a clouding of the lens of the eye, and that they appear gradually, and get worse with time. Cataracts can usually be corrected with surgery.

3. Loss of peripheral (side) vision can also be simulated. Have the boys extend their arms at shoulder level. Looking straight ahead, and starting with their arms as far back as possible, have the boys slowly move their arms forward until they can see their fingers. Tape a square of paper at eye-level on one side of the head. Again, have the boys look straight ahead and repeat the arm motion.

    - Can they see one hand sooner than the other? How much do they need to turn the head to see the other hand? **(O)**
    - How might this affect daily activities? What particular safety precautions might have to be taken? **(G)**

4. To simulate tunnel vision, punch a small hole (the smaller the better) about midway across and about 2 inches from the end of a sheet of letter-sized paper. Wrap the other ends of the paper around the sides of the boy's head to eliminate side vision. Line up the hole with the center of one eye. The Cub Scout closes the other eye and looks through the hole only.

    - What can be seen? Open the other eye. How difficult is it to focus on objects? **(O)**
    - How might one help a person who has tunnel vision? **(O)**

Mobility

Many people experience difficulty in moving around as they grow older. Sometimes one whole side is affected, or only certain joints may be involved. There are many different causes for such changes.

- How many can the boys think of? (e.g., diseases such as arthritis, side effects of medications, accidents, loss of calcium in the bones, etc.). To get started, talk about what they already know. **(O)**

Materials: Rubber gloves; ice cream sticks of various lengths (with any sharp edges covered with tape) a shoe with laces; an article of clothing with buttons; rolled newspapers; elastic bandages or dishtowels; canes; crutches; a wheelchair.

1. Have each Cub Scout put on the shoe and tie it; put on the clothing and button and unbutton it. Any problems? Now, have them put on the rubber gloves and try to do the same things. It is more difficult! Explain that some people may lose the sense of touch following a stroke or because of poor circulation.

2. To simulate joint stiffness (e.g., from arthritis), insert different lengths of ice cream sticks into three fingers, of the gloves (making sure that the sticks are behind the fingers, on the back side of the hand). Now try to tie the shoe and button and unbutton the clothing. It will be much harder!

- Have them imagine that each joint that couldn't move well was also painful. What would a person with this problem need to do to adapt? What might they do to make things easier? What gadgets (e.g., electric can-openers) are available that could help? **(O)**

3. Many disabled people have difficulty with major joints. A stiff joint can be simulated with a rolled-up newspaper tied on (not too tight!) with an elastic bandage or dishtowel.

- What does a stiff joint do to a person's "gait" (that is, the way he or she walks)? How even is it? How does it affect balance? **(G)**

Have the boys walk while leaning on each other for support. Have someone explain the correct use of a cane and crutches. Have the boys walk, using them for support.

- Which helped most? What are the problems involved? **(O)**
- How might they help someone who needed a cane or crutches? **(G)**

4. Try to borrow a wheelchair. (If this is not possible, designate any chair in the room as the wheelchair.) Have each boy take a turn sitting there for a specific amount of time while the group continues its activities.

- What happens to the boy in the wheelchair? Does the group always remember to include him? Have him describe what he sees from the chair. What happens to the dynamics of the group when one person is in a wheelchair? What can be done to help? **(G)**

Add another disability, such as blindness, by blindfolding the person in the wheelchair. What happens then? Be creative with this one. The boys will come up with a great many ideas of their own. Give them opportunities to express their feelings about their experiences.

Speech

Materials: Adhesive tape (a type that can be removed easily from the skin).

Often people who have had strokes or diseases affecting coordination will lose control of some of the muscles of the face and tongue. This makes it hard to speak clearly. Sometimes this is a permanent condition, and sometimes the muscles can be "retrained." It is especially frustrating when a speech problem affects the ability to communicate easily with others. Sometimes speech difficulties are caused by loss of teeth or poorly fitted dentures.

Take one piece of adhesive tape and cover half of each Cub Scout's mouth and stretch a second piece across the cheek. Try to have a normal conversation. Remind them that although they can remove the tape, a stroke victim remains that way.

- How did they feel when others could not understand them? **(F)**
- How might someone with a speech problem be helped to communicate with other people? Are there some signs that they might use? **(G)**

Memory Loss

Memory loss is difficult to simulate, but it is quite a common condition among the elderly. There are many causes of memory loss, but the effects are similar. Memory loss can be very bewildering to people on both sides of a conversation. A person who has a memory problem may repeat some things many times, and be unaware that they have just said the same thing. Or, they may forget that they have just met someone a few minutes before.

The den leader might pretend to have a loss of memory by repeating something she/he has just said, or by "forgetting" the boys' names or some other recent experience that they have all had.

- How do the boys react? Do they get angry? Suppose it happened over and over again; how would they react? **(F)**

Memory loss is often a problem for which there is no solution. It just requires a great deal of patience and understanding.

Relfecting

These are some questions that can be used with any of the activities.

- Does anyone have a friend or a relative with [this problem]? **(O)**
- If someone does, ask: How do you feel when you are around this person? How do you think the other person feels? Is it hard or easy for you to understand each other? Is it hard or easy to find things that you can do together? **(F)**

- Is it right to leave someone out of the "fun" the group is having because the person has a handicap? **(J)**
- How can we make everyone feel comfortable in the group? How can we make it possible for everyone to be part of the "action?" **(C)**

Followup

Invite some older neighbors or relatives of the Cub Scouts to a den or pack meeting. If they are willing and able, enlist them as friends and resources for the pack and dens. Children often long for information about their roots. Have their older friends talk about their own childhoods. Conversations about school experiences and how they celebrated holidays in days gone by are of interest to most, and a good way to get started. Find out what the boys can do for their older friends. (The pack's chartered organization may be able to suggest some older people who would enjoy getting to know the boys.)

Visit a nursing home. (You may want to choose a time other than near a holiday.) Before the first visit explain that some of the furniture and the odors there may be different from what they are used to in their own homes. If the nursing home has an "adopt a grandparent" program, take an active part on a continuing basis.

Remember older friends on birthdays and holidays with cards and simple gifts.

Caring and Sharing

This activity uses a mock court to deal with the issues of taking care of one's own things and respecting the property of other people.

Overview

American children get a lot of mixed messages about having, owning, and being responsible for "things." On the one hand, our culture encourages people to own things—the more, the better. On the other hand, we also encourage children to share what they have, and to respect the property of others. Teaching responsibility for the care of things is not the easiest part of raising children.

Adults often think youngsters of Cub Scout age are careless. In defense of young people, we might point out that over and above the mixed messages that adults send, there are some other ways that we encourage rather casual attitudes toward property. Some of them are:

- Many American children today have so many things (clothes, toys, books, and so forth) that the loss of some of them may not seem very great. They often have other things that can fill gaps, or they assume that someone will see to it that they get what they want.

- Many of their things, particularly toys, are so poorly made that even quite careful use does not prevent breakage. This makes it difficult for them to make connections between caring for things and keeping them in good condition.

- They do not yet understand what is involved in making things, or working to make money to buy or replace things. It is hard for boys to understand how much things cost and the amount of time someone must work to pay for them.

- They are just beginning to be able to consider other people's points of view and to be able to understand how another person might feel about having property damaged or destroyed.

Cub Scout Court is designed to help the boys think about the care of property and the consequences of carelessness or outright destruction.

Preparation

Cub Scout Court assumes that boys of Cub Scout- and Webelos Scout-age will have some idea of the way a court of law operates. Many of them will have watched such scenes on television. It might be useful to videotape a short court scene in advance. Show it at the beginning of the activity to help them understand some of the people and roles involved. Or, even better, the den might invite an attorney to come to the meeting to talk about how law courts work.

Materials: A small table and chair for the judge. A chair for the witness. Chairs for the members of the jury.

(If this activity is to be developed as a skit for presentation to a larger audience, you may want to add props such as a gavel, a robe for the judge, briefcases for the attorneys, and so forth.)

Group: Cub Scout Court works best with Webelos Scouts. (Some third-grade Bear Cub Scouts might be able to do it, but they would need a lot more preparation.) Two dens will probably be needed to fill all of the roles, including the jury. If a single den wants to prepare this activity for a pack meeting, the den members could fill the main roles themselves and choose the jury from the audience.

Characters: The activity will go more smoothly if the leader matches the number of characters to be involved to the number of boys available to play them. The following characters are required:

- **Plaintiff** (the person making the complaint)
- **Defendant** (the person accused, or against whom the complaint is made)
- **Prosecuting attorney** (the person who presents arguments on the side of the plaintiff)
- **Defense attorney** (the person who presents arguments on the side of the defendant)
- **Witnesses** (people who testify in support of one side of the argument)—as needed.
- **Jury** (a group of peers chosen to listen to both sides of the issue and decide on a verdict)
- **Judge** (the person who presides over the trial and sets the sentence if the defendant is found guilty)

Here are two cases to help you get started. (The boys might prefer to make up one of their own to act out.)

1. One night, Jason forgot to put his bike in the garage as he was supposed to. While it was sitting out, someone stole it. He needs a bike to do his paper route, but his father is refusing to buy him another one.

    Jason is making a complaint against his father, claiming that he is being stingy and unfair.

    Jason's father is making a counter-complaint against Jason, claiming that he has been careless and does not deserve another bike.

    Each attorney must see that his client's arguments are heard before the court. The jury must decide the case in favor of either Jason or his father. The judge must decide on an appropriate sentence for the losing party.

2. The Cub Scouts are playing ball in the parking lot next to Mr. Carter's house. Suddenly, the ball goes over the curb and into his garden. In their enthusiasm to score, several of the boys follow the ball and realize, too late, that they have trampled down the prized flowers that Mr. Carter has been caring for all summer.

    Mr. Carter makes a complaint against the Cub Scouts for destroying his flower bed.

    The Cub Scouts' attorney pleads that it was just an accident and that "boys will be boys."

    Each side must present its case. If the jury finds the Cub Scouts guilty, the judge must suggest a plan for paying back or making restitution to Mr. Carter for the loss of his flowers.

Action

As noted above, Cub Scout Court may be done as a simple role-playing activity in a single meeting, or may be prepared as a skit to be performed before an audience of other Cub Scouts and/or adults. If done as role-play only, one case is enough for one meeting. Even fifth-graders are likely to lose interest after the first one.

Choosing roles: The easiest way to choose parts for the role-play is to write the name of each one on a slip of paper and have each boy draw one. There should be a part for each boy. (Witnesses for one side or the other can be added or the size of the jury adjusted to make things come out even.)

Conducting Court: Give the attorneys and their clients about 5 minutes to prepare their cases. (The others should have something to keep them busy during this time.)

When ready, the judge calls the court to order. The prosecuting attorney opens the case, and the defense attorney follows. Give each side a set amount of time (no more than 2 to 4 minutes) to present his case. Witnesses may then be called and cross-examined. When both sides have presented their arguments, the judge sends the case to the jury for deliberation and a decision. The jury may hold its discussion in secret (as in a real courtroom) or in front of the group. When they have decided the case, they tell their decision to the judge. The judge then pronounces the sentence.

The keys to the success of this activity are good preparation (making sure that the boys understand their roles and what goes on in a court of law), not letting the trial go on too long, and not trying more than one case during a meeting.

Reflecting

Leaders have expressed surprise at how well their Cub Scouts were able to develop both sides of the argument, once they really got into it. They really were able to act from the points of view of the characters they were playing. In reflecting following the skit, the role-players had a chance to explain why they said or did something during the activity. They also discussed the fairness of the jury's verdict and the sentence of the judge, and suggested other possibilities. Some questions that help the discussion might be:

- Was it hard to pretend you were a person at a real trial? **(O)**
- How did it feel trying to explain your side to the judge and jury? **(F)**
- Was the "verdict" of the jury fair? How about the sentence: was it fair? **(J)**
- Are there some times when we could use a pretend "court" to help us understand some problems we have in our den? **(C)**

Followup

It may happen that a real instance of carelessness and/or destruction of property comes to the attention of the Cub Scouts at some time during the year. It may or may not actually involve the den members. Turning the situation into a courtroom drama may help the group to identify and understand some of the issues involved. If the case is a real one, and the den members are directly involved, holding court on the issue could be a way of helping them discuss the problem. By using the formal courtroom way of presenting opposite points of view, the boys may be less emotional in deciding their guilt or innocence in the matter. The court process could also be used to involve them in working out a real solution to the problem. The solution could include a plan for restitution, if the circumstances call for one.

The leader should not attempt to use role-playing in a real situation unless it can be guaranteed that the drama will not turn into a fight, or result in scapegoating one or more members of the group.

Consumer Alert

This activity helps boys analyze commercial messages on television and in printed advertisements.

Overview

The average young American may see some 20,000 television commercials each year. In addition to TV, there are advertisements in comic books, newspapers, and magazines—all begging for his or her dollars. And youngsters do have dollars! In 1989, 4- to 12-year-olds were a $60 billion market! Children in this age group had $9 billion of their own money to save or spend as they pleased.

Of course, the reason that so much consumerism is aimed directly at children is that research has shown that youngsters do respond to advertising, particularly when they are very young. Some psychologists feel that children become cynical when they discover that reality does not live up to the promises made in commercials. Although many Cub Scouts and Webelos Scouts may already have become skeptics, from time to time the boys undoubtedly will see something that they "just have to have" among the flood of advertisements and commercials—particularly around the gift-giving holidays.

HIDDEN MESSAGES

Ads from Magazines or Newspapers

The idea behind this activity is to help the boys discover the hidden message behind what advertisements say. For example, the endorsement of beer by popular athletes is sending out the message: "If you drink this, you may be popular and good at sports, too." Or, the beautiful woman standing next to the car in an ad, is suggesting the message: "Drive a car like this, and beautiful women will fall all over you." In addition to sending messages that will not be true for a good many beer drinkers or car owners, such advertisements can keep stereotypes alive.

In the case of the beer commercial, a deeper message that boys can pick up is that they have to drink to be popular athletes. In the case of the car, boys may get the idea that they need a flashy one if they want girls to be their friends.

Probably the deepest messages are beyond the understanding of many Cub Scouts, but they should be able to grasp some of the subtleties of advertising. Further, having discovered the hidden message, the boys should be able to make a decision as to whether the ad is "fair," or "unfair." The leader needs to be a careful listener; boys may see quite different hidden messages than he or she does. Keep the discussion open.

Preparation

Ask each boy to bring a magazine from home—one that contains a number of advertisements that can be cut out. The leader may prefer to supply the ads. There should be enough so that each boy has two or three ads. To guarantee fairness, they could be numbered, and slips of paper with the corresponding numbers placed in a bowl to be drawn by the boys.

If the ads are to be used at another meeting (see below), they should also be trimmed and mounted on heavier paper to keep them from being torn.

Action

Each boy takes one ad from the set, and looks at it for a minute or so, trying to answer these questions:

- What is the ad telling you to buy?

- Why do the words say you should buy it?
- What is the picture all about?
- Does the picture contain a hidden message?
- If so, what is it?

When each boy thinks he has discovered a hidden message, he may want to write it down, if he can't keep it in his head.

Then have the boys exchange ads with another member of the group and repeat the process. (A system, such as having each boy do his exchanging with the boy two chairs to the right, may make things go more smoothly.) Then have them compare the messages each found, and discuss them with the group.

Ask the whole group to vote on whether or not they think that each ad is fair or unfair. Discuss (briefly) why they voted the way they did.

This activity may move fairly quickly; some groups will want to do it with more than one set of advertisements.

Television Commercials: Your den may wish to start with TV commercials, or to move on to them after looking at the magazine advertisements.

Preparation

Before the meeting, record several video commercials (about five). These should be commercials that are aimed at young viewers—perhaps from a morning cartoon show or a popular sitcom.

Provide each boy with a pencil and paper. Many youngsters are not very keen on doing written work during den meetings; the leaders should decide whether to simply ask the boys to discuss their ideas rather than write them down. If so, it is good to have a pre-recorded commercial for each member of the group so that each boy will have a chance to lead part of the discussion.

Action

Show the commercials, one at a time. Ask the boys to think about what they have seen, using the same list of questions given above. When a boy thinks he has found a hidden message, he should write it down.

After all of the commercials have been shown, share the hidden messages. Vote on whether each commercial is fair or unfair, or have a different boy lead the discussion of each commercial. You might want to have someone serve as scribe to keep a record of the various messages found.

Reflecting

Young people who watch a lot of TV are remarkably familiar with commercials, and often have favorites. Sometimes boys also have commercials that they dislike. As a group, discuss some of the commercials that they like and dislike to see whether the hidden messages have anything to do with how the boys feel about them. Some other questions you might use are:

- Do ads in magazines and TV commercials influence the way we think? **(O)**
- How do you feel when you see an advertisement that sends you the message that "to be cool, you need to drink alcohol?" **(F)**
- Is it fair for companies that want to sell their products to try to make people believe things that are not exactly true? **(J)**
- What can people do to tell companies that their advertisements and commercials are not fair? **(C)**

Followup

Sharing. Den members may want to share their findings with another den or the whole pack. At a meeting, pin up a series of ads. Give each boy a recording form with a line for each ad. After explaining how to analyze an ad, tell the boys to write down the hidden message that they find in each one. If they want to make a game out of it, assign a point for each message found and add them up. The high-scoring den wins.

Role-Playing. Acting out magazine ads or commercials can provide more insights into the hidden messages they contain.

Magazine Ads. Have on hand several magazine ads; each should have several people pictured. Choose an ad and assign, or draw numbers for the role of each person in the picture. Give the actors a few minutes to plan a skit in which they:

- Show what the people in the ad were doing and saying just before the picture was taken.
- Strike the pose that the camera caught in the ad.
- Show what the people in the ad were doing and saying just after the picture was taken.

TV Commercials. Act out the TV commercial, but not as it was shown. Some ideas for changes are:

- Reverse the parts played by male and female actors. What does this say about stereotyping of roles?
- Continue the action past what was presented on TV to show what would most likely happen to the people in real life, or if the hidden message came true.

Differences

Helps Cub Scouts explore their attitudes toward differences in people (gender, racial or ethnic backgrounds, physical appearance, and economic status).

Overview

Americans pride themselves on being the most diverse nation in the world. There were already many different Native American people living here before Europeans came. Since then, groups from every part of the globe have been added. In addition to physical differences such as height, body build, and skin color, immigrants to America brought other differences, such as language, political attitudes, artistic and social traditions, and religious beliefs—to name but a few. All of these differences have been combined as the rich cultural patchwork we like to call "the American way of life."

People used to talk about the United States becoming a "melting pot" where old-country differences should and would blend and disappear. After more than 200 years of being a nation, we are beginning to feel that this is not going to happen. Rather, we are learning to appreciate our differences and see them as rich sources of new ideas and creative solutions to problems.

However, even though it is part of the American way of life to talk about "equality for all," old attitudes have not always kept pace with the newer laws that guarantee civil rights. Today, access to justice, education, and jobs may still too often be related to differences that people are born with, such as gender, skin color, national origin, and even attractiveness.

By the time boys are old enough to be Cub Scouts, they have been picking up attitudes toward differences in people for several years. They learn their attitudes from their families, their friends, the media, and who knows where else.

As soon as children can recognize themselves as individuals, distinct from other people (at around age 2), they start making comparisons. These comparisons can develop into beliefs about differences between "them" and "us." For example, research with pre-schoolers found that both white and non-white toddlers had already learned a bias that favored whites. By elementary school age, children also have developed stereotyped thinking related to such differences as gender, physical appearance, and age.

These attitudes towards members of various groups can be found in the put-down names that boys call each other. Even though they don't always know what these names mean, the message begins to come through that being one

isn't good. By the time they do know what the words mean, negative attitudes (sometimes unconscious) are often already associated with the words.

Prejudice can be thought of as a social disease. People catch it from other people. No one or no group is immune from prejudging others. However, we can recognize and build up resistance to prejudices in ourselves and help children to do the same. Positive, flexible attitudes toward other people are rooted in a strong, positive image of ourselves. Self-assured youngsters are not threatened by differences and are open to the new experiences that differences make possible. Self-confident children learn not to take negative cultural myths about other people seriously. They make up their own minds about people as individuals, not as members of a category.

Preparation

This activity, called One Potato, My Potato, is designed to help Scouts discover that each member of a group is a special individual. This activity can be done with groups of about 8 to 20 boys.

Materials: A large bag containing potatoes. If doing this with a single den, have one potato for each boy and adult. (For a larger group, have one potato for each two boys.)

Action

Ask the boys whether they agree with the statement, "All potatoes are alike." (If there is a difference of opinion, write down how many are on each side of the issue.)

Roll the potatoes out of the bag and ask each boy (or pair of boys) to take one. Ask them to look carefully at the potatoes and "make friends" with them so they can introduce their new "friends" to the rest of the group. They should give the potatoes names. (They don't all have to be male!) Give the group one minute of silence for the getting-acquainted process.

After the silent time, begin by introducing your own potato to the group. Tell a little story about it. You might comment on certain physical characteristics (perhaps the little dent it has because it grew next to a stone, or all of the eyes it has to see in every direction).

Then in turn, give each boy (or pair) a chance to introduce his potato to the group, and to describe some of its unique features. When all potatoes have been introduced, ask the boys to put their potatoes back into the bag. (Observe to see if there is any difference in the way the boys handle their potatoes now, from the way they did earlier. If so, comment on this.)

Then ask if the boys think they could find their "friends" again.

Roll the potatoes out of the bag a second time, and ask them to find their friends. (People who have done this with lots of groups report that they always can.)

Ask them again whether they agree with the statement: "All potatoes are alike." Has anyone changed his mind since the first time the question was asked? Go around the group and ask each boy (or pair) to tell about one way that his potato is different from all the others.

Reflecting

Begin to wind down the activity by thinking of some similarities between potatoes and people.

- How are potatoes like people? **(O)**

Divide the boys into pairs and give them 2 to 3 minutes for each to discover something unique about the other person. (Stress the positive, such as a hobby, favorite food, a place he has been, etc.) Have each boy introduce his partner to the group by describing the unique feature that he has discovered.

- Do we (or other people) sometimes look at certain kinds of people—members of a particular ethnic group, fat kids, or Cub Scouts, for example, and say "Oh, they're all alike?" **(G)**
- What does this tell about the person who says that? Does it mean that he has not bothered to get to know that person as an individual? **(J)**
- How does it feel when you are the one called a name? **(F)**

If there is time, and interest is still there, the group may want to go on to talk about similarities. Although each person is in some way unique, it is sometimes important to know about ways that they are similar. Go back to the potatoes.

- Ask the boys if they can think of ways that their potatoes are similar. **(G)**

Make a list of the kinds of similarities they discover. Then look at each of the potatoes and decide how many groups (from the list) each potato might fit into. Use guiding questions (for example, "What are some ways people are similar or alike?") until the boys understand the point of this part of the discussion: People, like potatoes, can be grouped in many different ways.

- Are there times when we enjoy being like other people? Are there times when we want to be different? Talk about some of the reasons for the answers that the boys give. **(C)**

The One Potato, My Potato has been adapted from an activity in the *Prejudice Book,* by David Shiman. We wish to thank Dr. Carol Wirtschafter and the Anti-Defamation League of B'nai B'rith for permission to adapt this activity for the Ethics in Action program.

Followup

Celebrate Differences. Find out what is the same and what is different in the ways that people of various religious or national backgrounds celebrate holidays. Try to learn some of the songs or make some of the foods associated with the different holiday traditions.

Start a collection of the way people say things in different languages. You might start with words like "friend," "hello," or "thank you" and go on from there. Add new ones to your collection as you have a chance.

Make New Friends. There are still a lot of newcomers to America each year. Many of them are children. Some come with their own families while others come alone, to be adopted into new families. Many of them are coming as refugees from war-torn countries. Sometimes when they start school, they do not speak English, and know almost nothing about American ways of doing things. Talk about what the Cub Scouts or Webelos Scouts could do to help, then do it! (It would be best to talk with the newcomer's family before going ahead, however.)

Role-Play. Prejudice often shows up in name-calling, or simply in the ways we talk about various groups of people. Have the boys recall some examples from their own experiences. Role-play ways the Scouts might act to fight against prejudice when they see it.

Overcoming. Learn some of the songs of the civil rights movement such as "We Shall Overcome." Who sang these songs and why? Do we still sing them today? Are there other places in the world where they sing them? What do these people have in common with the Americans who sang the songs?

Learn about some Americans who found prejudice and discrimination blocking their paths, yet overcame these obstacles to reach their goals. Your local librarian can help.

Glossary

These terms are useful for discussing relationships among people:

Culture. The traditions, customs, and ways of living that belong to a certain group.

Prejudice. Judging people without really knowing anything about them just because they belong to a certain group.

Discrimination. Keeping someone from something they want to do or join because they belong to a certain group. (This is not the same as disliking someone after you get to know him or her.)

Stereotype. A way of thinking based on the belief that all members of a certain group are alike and will act the same way. (Be sensitive in using this term. There is some research to suggest that unless the term *stereotype* is very carefully explained, young concrete thinkers of Cub Scout age may confuse the stereotype with what is real.)

Chauvinism. An exaggerated belief that one's own group is superior to others. This is a kind of stereotype, too.

Racism. The belief that human abilities are determined by race. This belief usually results in stereotyping and in discrimination.

Sexism. The belief that human abilities are determined by gender. This also leads to stereotyping and discrimination.

Scapegoating. Blaming someone for something that he or she didn't do because of the group they belong to.

Fire! Fire!

This activity explores the responsible use of fire. It deals with the kinds of decisions regarding fire that Cub Scouts are likely to face.

Overview

People seem to have been fascinated with fire since the beginning of time. Bringing the forces of fire under control so that it could be used for cooking, heating, and producing steam were turning points in the long development of human civilization. The amazing forces of uncontrolled fire have inspired many of our rituals. At various times and places in history, fire itself has been worshiped.

It is no wonder that young people find fire fascinating. However, this interest can lead to dangerous experiments with matches, lighters, and stoves. Children set about 70,000 fires a year. Most of these fires are not set in a deliberate attempt to destroy property. Rather, they happen when children are playing with fire and lose control over it. For a small number of children, fire may become a way of expressing anger, or fire may be a cry for attention to needs that are not being met. Research shows that children are more likely to abuse fire when they are trying to cope with major upheavals in their lives. Youngsters who abuse fire need a great deal more help than can be provided in a Cub Scout pack. These children should be referred to professional therapists.

Children must learn that anything that will produce fire is a tool. Tools that start fires include matches, lighters, stoves, or even magnifying glasses. Like all tools, they must be used carefully, and in appropriate ways. Many fire educators believe that programs like Scouting, that emphasize correct fire-building and fire-safety techniques, provide important ways to make this lesson clear to young people. By the time a boy has worked to prepare a safe area, gathered the kindling and wood, and placed these materials so that they will burn, the actual lighting of the match is somewhat of an anticlimax. Lighting the fire is seen as but one step in the total process of using fire *for a purpose*. Cub Scouting books offer instruction on fire safety and guidance regarding when youngsters are ready to light fires themselves.

Children today are often without adult supervision. Studies of the way children spend the hours right after school have found that more than half of fourth- to sixth-graders are usually home alone or under the care of a slightly older sibling. It is at these times in particular that young people must be prepared to act in a responsible way where fire is concerned. Many schools are working with local fire departments to teach youngsters fire safety. Some

communities use the Learn Not to Burn curriculum developed by the National Fire Protection Association. This is a carefully designed fire prevention and safety education program for school children. These lessons take into account the fact that levels of cognitive and moral development differ according to age level, and each age level has its own hazards associated with fire.

FIRE HAZARDS

Boys of Cub Scout and Webelos Scout age are highly active physically. They also have a lively curiosity. Further, they have the cognitive and motor skills to put their curiosity to work. Sometimes the things that boys this age can think up amaze us—and may dismay us! The particular hazards of fire for this age group are related to the characteristics of normal development. Some of these hazards are:

1. They are likely to play with matches, lighters, and other fire-starting devices.
2. They may get too close to an open fire, causing clothing to ignite.
3. They may be the victims of smoking carelessness—their own, or that of adults.
4. They can be easily influenced by peers because they have a strong desire to conform in group situations.
5. They do not yet have the abstract reasoning ability to predict the likely outcomes of their experiments or actions.

The ways that we try to teach boys about fire safety must take these developmental factors into account. Cub Scouting can offer youngsters a peer group where responsible use of fire is the right thing to do. Being responsible frequently involves learning to make good decisions.

DECIDING ON THE SAFE WAY

Fire-Starting Equipment. It goes without saying that matches, lighters (particularly disposables), and such objects *should* be kept out of the reach of children. The truth is that even when proper care is taken at home, youngsters are likely to find them in other places. Some boys may take matches or lighters from the safe places where adults have put them. Sometimes even adults who are usually careful have moments of carelessness. Thus, it is safer to assume that young people will have access to tools that can start fires. We must teach them rules to cover such situations. These rules are:

1. **Do not** play with matches, lighters, or any other tool for lighting fires.

2. If there is any danger of younger children reaching tools that can start fires, they must be put out of reach.
3. If they find tools that can start fires, boys should take them to an adult; boys should not try to see if the tools work.

Open Fires. Active children are often careless. Many of the fabrics in the clothing children wear burn easily. If a child gets too close to an open fire, his clothing may catch fire. When clothing catches fire, some children instinctively start to run. Of course, this just makes the flames worse. There is only one rule to follow in this situation:

"STOP, DROP, AND ROLL!"

"Stop, drop and roll" means that the child must **stop** immediately. Then, he must **drop** to the ground, covering his face with his hands. Then he must **roll** on the ground until the flames are out. This exercise must be practiced. Even if the boys have learned it in school, it is good to reinforce this important safety rule in Cub Scout settings. Boys should be reminded of it as part of the preparation for any cookout. The drawing at the end of this chapter shows the "stop, drop, and roll" technique. It may be reproduced so that each youngster has one to take home to show to his family.

Smoking. "Smokers need watchers!" More than half of home fires are caused by careless smokers. Children can be encouraged to be detectives of carelessness. Cub Scout fire-safety activities must be discussed with parents who, it is hoped, will support the detective activity of their youngsters to make their homes safer.

Peer Pressure. The middle childhood years are a time when children try to conform to the behavior of people they like. They want and need to be accepted by peers. Even children with normal levels of self-esteem can become involved in dangerous activities when they are in a group. Youngsters egg each other on. In such situations, they rarely stop to think about possible consequences. Sometimes before they really know what they are doing, children can create a very dangerous crisis.

Children of this age follow their own rules against "telling on" themselves or each other. What this can mean is that they simply run away from a fire after they have started it. They don't report the fire. By the time someone else discovers the fire, it can be too late to control the flames. While we hope that Cub Scouts would use positive peer pressure to keep their peers from setting fires in the first place, there are no guarantees. Therefore, Cub Scouts must know how to report a fire. They need to know these rules, too:

1. Do not play with fire; try to prevent your friends or younger children from playing with fire.
2. Know how to report a fire.
3. Never turn in a false alarm at an alarm box. Never call in a false report of a fire.

Many local fire prevention bureaus use the "Fire Stop" program with children who have been involved in setting a fire.

Understanding Consequences. Watching fire trucks respond to an alarm is exciting. Children have been known to turn in false alarms just for their own fun. Youngsters must be helped to understand why false alarms are dangerous. If firefighters are answering a false alarm, they can't respond to a real emergency. Furthermore, every time the equipment leaves the fire station, it costs the community money.

Action

The activities that follow involve both safety precautions that youngsters can take, and ways of impressing them with the seriousness of uncontrolled fire.

Field Trips. As budgets have become tighter, some schools have cut out field trips for elementary students. Other schools still have field trips or have other special events during national Fire Prevention Week (the second week of October—the anniversary of the Great Chicago Fire). Leaders should try to avoid duplicating what is being done in school. If the den goes on a field trip, the boys should be encouraged to ask questions and talk about their own experiences.

Fire Station. Even though the boys may have been to a fire station, going in a small den-size group may make it possible to see and learn more. Trips should be arranged well in advance, and the leaders should discuss specifically what they hope to see and do. Insurance regulations will probably make it impossible for the boys to try out equipment. (When they get older, they can join a fire safety Explorer post, if interested.) Some of the things that you might wish them to see:

- **A firefighter dressed in full uniform.** The full gear totally covers the firefighter's body. This can be very frightening to youngsters the first time they see it. Some scared children have even hidden from the firefighters who were trying to rescue them.

- **Different types of vehicles.** Most stations have equipment for pumping water and for reaching fires above the ground. Some may have paramedical emergency vehicles and the "jaws of life" for getting injured people out of wrecks.

The firefighters who talk to the boys will undoubtedly reinforce fire safety rules, the dangers of false alarms, and so forth. Webelos Scouts, particularly, will be impressed with how much equipment costs, and how much it costs each time the company responds to an alarm. These cost figures might be converted into how many bikes the same amount of money would buy, or how many trips to the amusement park that sum would cover.

Preparedness at Home. Parents will, of course, know of the field trip that is planned, but leaders may wish to remind them that this experience will open up an opportunity to discuss what the boys have seen and learned. The field trip can be a stimulus for working out a home-safety program, including a family emergency evacuation plan.

This plan should be practiced. Other family activities may include checking smoke detectors, looking for hazards and removing them, and reviewing safety procedures every time an open fire is used.

The best place to start for fire-safety information, planning field trips, etc., is your local fire station or fire prevention bureau.

Service for a Hospital Burn Unit. Recovery from burn injuries is a long, painful process, full of discouragement. There are often long periods of hospitalization followed by months of therapy. Cub Scouts and Webelos Scouts can help burn patients by collecting books (new or used), and by collecting pictures that patients can cut out and make into scrap books. It would be good to include safe scissors, white glue, and blank scrap books, too. All such activities should be planned in advance with hospital volunteer service personnel.

Reflecting

Specific points of discussion will vary according to what the den has actually seen and experienced. In general, the reflecting time should be used to try to reinforce safety, prevention, preparedness, and personal responsibility. Some questions that might be asked are:

- What was something you learned that you didn't know before? **(O)**
- What do you think about children or adults who start fires on purpose? **(J)**

I Know How To Stop, Drop & Roll

Hard Lessons

This activity simulates learning disabilities and underscores the need for understanding children and adults with learning problems.

Overview

What do **Leonardo da Vinci, Albert Einstein, Thomas Edison, Hans Christian Andersen, Cher,** and **Bruce Jenner** have in common? Give up?

They all experienced **learning disabilities** in childhood. Leonardo's notebooks were penned in mirror writing; Einstein was dyslexic; his teachers labeled him a slow learner. Edison's failures caused his parents to withdraw him from school and have him taught at home. Danish schools were no kinder to Hans Christian Andersen, who was considered awkward and immature. Cher still has difficulty reading scripts and, like many learning-disabled people, compensates with an excellent memory. Olympic decathlon gold-medalist Jenner was also dyslexic. This is but a short list of individuals, famous for their achievements in widely different fields, who have overcome early learning problems. There are millions more like them, successfully pursuing all walks of life. Unfortunately, there are also many millions like them whose disabilities have gone unrecognized. All their lives, disabilities continue to hold them back from success.

The subject of learning disabilities is highly complex—too complex to try to cover here in any but a very sketchy way. Historical accounts suggest that there have always been children who seemed to be bright in some ways, but were unable to keep up with their peers. More often than not, such children were considered lazy, uncooperative, or even just plain stupid. It has only been within the past 20 years or so that systematic research has been done in this area. There is still a great deal to be learned, but some of the things we know are:

- Children with learning disabilities are not dumb, as they are often labeled; many are highly gifted.

- Although there are patterns of disabilities, every child is unique.

- Until very recently, more boys than girls were identified as having learning disabilities, apparently because boys' behavior was more disruptive in the classroom. However, it now appears that about equal numbers of boys and girls have learning difficulties.

- With proper diagnosis and treatment, sometimes lasting years, most disabilities can be overcome or bypassed so that children can get on successfully with their lives.

- There is a strong relationship between undiagnosed learning disabilities and juvenile delinquency, adult illiteracy, and adult crime.

Learning disabilities are believed to be a result of lagging development in a child's nervous system. No single cause has been isolated. Learning disabilities sometimes seem to run in families. They have also been associated with such factors as difficult pregnancies, difficult births, mothers' drug or alcohol use during pregnancy, malnutrition both before and after birth, childhood diseases such as meningitis or encephalitis, head injuries and lead poisoning—among others. There simply are no easy answers. The term "learning disabilities" covers a variety of the consequences of developmental immaturity. The U.S. government has provided the following legal definition:

> ...a disorder in one or more of the basic psychological processes involved in understanding or in using language, spoken or written, which disorder may manifest itself in imperfect ability to listen, think, speak, read, write, spell, or do mathematical calculations.

This definition suggests the incredible variety in learning disabilities. Note that it does not include either mental retardation or emotional disturbance. Children with learning disabilities have been described as being a little like a jig-saw puzzle where a few of the pieces are missing. Sometimes the pieces eventually show up, and sometimes they don't. Learning-disabled youngsters experience intense frustration in trying to make sense of and gain control over their lives. Characteristics shared by some learning disabled children (but not all of them) include:

- Unable to concentrate; impulsive; will say whatever pops into his or her head, whether it is appropriate or not

- Once he or she starts something, it may be very difficult to get him or her to stop

- Does not keep up with his or her peers in developing reading, writing, and/or mathematical skills

- Has poor social skills; is argumentative and is often defensive; may tell fabulous tales of which he or she is the hero. (Other children rather quickly learn to reject such stories.)

- Poor eye-hand coordination; may have trouble with skills like catching a ball or tying shoes; may appear clumsy and often bump into things

- Likes routines; is upset with changes

- Has a level of activity that is different; some may be hyperactive and others may seem lethargic when compared to peers

- Disorganized; loses or forgets things; has poor memory for some things, but not others (for example, may deny, with absolute conviction, having said something that everyone else heard him or her say)

Any of these characteristics, alone or in combination, can be a source of much difficulty for a child. The fact that others seem sure that he or she is doing it on purpose makes it particularly hard. Working and living with children with learning disabilities can be extremely distressing to some parents, teachers, peers, and others. Learning disabilities have been associated with child abuse. Sometimes it is very difficult to determine whether the abuse is a cause or a consequence of the learning problem and turbulent relationships with family or others. Children with learning disabilities are often very bright and may feel a need to strike back at the world that misunderstands them. Children with learning disabilities can be extremely disruptive.

Even though much progress has been made in identifying and helping children with learning disabilities, some slip through the system unknown. There are many sources of help available. See "Resources."

Preparation

The activities that follow try to simulate learning disabilities. Some form of failure is built into each one. The activities are designed to give Cub Scouts a sense of the frustration that children with learning disabilities often feel when trying to do quite ordinary things. Some leaders have found it hard to help the boys make the connection between the activity and a learning disability. Two factors seem to help make this activity successful: doing only one or two parts in a single meeting, and guiding the discussion that follows each action.

Some general things to keep in mind as you prepare for reflecting after the activity are:

- Try to move the discussion away from such words as "dumb" or "stupid" to words like "frustrated," "just can't seem to do this," or "it didn't come out the way I thought it would."

- Even though there may be some things that a person with learning disabilities cannot do easily, there are always a great many more that he or she can do well. Failure in one thing does not cancel out the possibility of success in others.

- Failure to do the tasks in these games does not affect the sort of person a boy is. He is the same person, whether he can do them or not.

Research has shown that consistent relationships with caring adults and peers are essential to the success of youngsters working to overcome their disabilities. The Cub Scout den can provide a supportive and helpful group of friends for a youngster with learning disabilities. About 10 percent of all children have some form of learning problem, so it is quite likely that one or more of the boys in a den will be learning disabled. Several leaders who were aware that one of the boys had a problem reported they invited his parents and/or the school's special education teacher to participate in the den meeting where some of these activities were done.

Action

SCRAMBLED WORDS

Materials: Make a copy of figure 1 for each Cub Scout.

Figure 1 contains the Cub Scout Promise and the Law of the Pack written as children with learning disabilities commonly see printed words. Of course, no single child would experience all of these distortions.

Activity: See how long it takes to figure out what it says.

"MIRROR, MIRROR."

Materials: one mirror for each two boys in the group. (Square or rectangular mirrors work best; any sharp edges should be covered by masking tape.) A copy of one of the words in figure 2 cut out and taped about 3 to 4 inches from the bottom edge of the mirror; pencil and paper (with lines works best) for each pair.

Activity: Divide the boys into pairs. One boy holds the mirror (as still as possible) while the other boy writes. The writer sits at a table while his partner holds the mirror upright near the top edge of the paper. Looking into the mirror (not at his hand or at the paper), the writer tries to copy what he sees in the mirror. When he has finished, he may look at what he has written. When the first writers have finished, reverse positions so that all boys have turns. Compare the mirror writing done by the boys with some of the mistakes that are in figure 1.

We found that "Mirror, Mirror" worked best with older boys. For younger boys, writing is such a new and, often, hard-won skill that they seem to be unable to risk error, and therefore must "cheat" by looking at their hands.

HIGH-MINDED ART

Materials: Drawing paper and a pencil or crayon, and a surface for writing (stiff cardboard or a fairly thick magazine will do) for each boy.

Activity: Figures 3 and 4 contain simple outline drawings. Hold one up so that all can see it. Each boy puts the paper on the writing surface and then puts both on top of his head. He tries to draw what he sees. Compare the artwork results.

Variation: In the same manner, have each Cub Scout try to write his name.

ALPHABET RACE

Materials: Pencil and paper for each boy.

Activity: With the preferred hand (the hand the boy normally uses for writing), have each boy write down as many letters of the alphabet as he can in 15 seconds. Now switch to the nonpreferred hand, and do the same thing. Compare the number of letters written with each hand. (There will be a lot of variation in the numbers of letters written by each boy. This is not a race to see who writes down the most letters, but a race between each boy's own right and left hands.)

FREE THROW

Materials: Two small bean bags, a wastebasket, and two pieces of rope or very heavy string about 3 feet long to serve as markers.

Activity 1. Using the rope, make a free-throw line behind which the players must stand. Set the empty wastebasket about 10 feet from the line. Have boys line up behind the line. Each one gets two chances to make a basket throwing the beanbags underhand, with his preferred (writing) hand. Count the number of baskets the whole group makes on this round. On the second round, switch to the nonpreferred hand and repeat the process. Compare the scores for the two rounds.

Activity 2. This variation should be done only where space permits. Using one piece of rope, make a free-throw line behind which the players must stand. On the first round, have each boy use his preferred hand and take a turn throwing one bag overhand as far as he can. Set the second piece of rope as a marker at the point that represents the shortest distance that anyone threw. On the second round, have each boy throw one bag overhand with his nonpreferred hand. How many went over the line?

We wish to thank Beth Emshoff and Phyllis Metcalf of the University of Minnesota, Dr. Julie Gilligan of the National Center for Learning Disabilities, and the Minnesota Association for Children and Adults with Learning Disabilities for help with the design of this activity.

Reflecting

- How did you feel when you tried to do a good job on this activity? **(F)**

- Would frustrated be a better word to describe how you felt, rather than saying you felt dumb, or stupid? Why? **(J)**

- Are you the same person, or a different person, because you could not do this activity well? Would this be the same, or different for someone who had a learning disability? **(J)**

- Think about what it must be like to feel frustrated every time you tried to do a certain thing that other kids seem to have no trouble with. After a while, what do you think you might do? **(G)**

- How could you help someone who was having problems doing one of these tasks? If you couldn't really help him or her, are there some ways you could make him feel better? **(G)**

- Can you think of someone who has difficulty doing one thing, but is really good at doing something else? How could you help this person feel good about the things he or she can do? **(C)**

```
   I romi  ot bo my des
 ot bo my but ot Go  anb
         my ountr,
    ot  elq  oths  eopl,
     anb ot ode  the
      La  fo  the  ac⅄.




  The  ud cou   ollows A⅄el.
  The  ud cou   elp  the  og.
     The  back  elp  the
        ud cou  ⅂ow.
  The  ud cou  iges   oobwil.
```

1 SCRAMBLED WORDS - Make a copy for each boy

MAY BE REPRODUCED

CUB SCOUTS

WEBELOS

2 "MIRROR, MIRROR" - Make enough copies for group; Cut out word-strips and tape to mirrors.

3 HIGHER ART

MAY BE REPRODUCED

4 HIGHER ART

Kindness Counts

These activities stress responsibility to animals, both at home and in the wild.

Overview

People have shared the world with animals since the dawn of human time. They have actually lived together, however, for a much shorter time — perhaps a few thousand years. The first domesticated animals seem to have been dogs and geese. Both of these animals are often given credit for having great loyalty and intelligence (although not in human form). In return for the freedom they have lost, humans have provided domestic animals with food, shelter, and protection from their natural enemies. Families today can choose from a wide range of household pets. Each type of pet, however, has special needs.

Most children are kind to animals most of the time. Many parents see pet care as a way to teach their youngsters about compassion for others. In a society like ours that provides few nurturing role models for boys, owning a pet may be particularly important. Caring for pets provides experience in providing for the needs of a dependent, defenseless creature. There is evidence that having pets makes a difference for some men. Recent research with young first-time fathers found that those who owned and were attached to a dog also felt more comfortable with their babies, were happier, and felt more competent in their new roles.

In general, children's failures with their pets involve not keeping to schedules of feeding, watering, and giving them exercise. Such slip-ups are more likely to be caused by the child's immaturity than by a deliberate attempt to harm the animal. Cruelty to pets of any kind, persistent teasing, or inhumane treatment of animals can be a signal that a child has serious problems. Such signals should not be ignored.

There are several kinds of animals that will be of particular interest to Cub Scouts and Webelos Scouts:

- Domestic pets
- Wild animals in the city or suburb
- Wild animals living in the country or in wilderness
- Endangered species

All animals have needs for respect and humane treatment from people.

Animal Pursuit is a game to help boys learn more about the lives of animals. It is hoped that such knowledge will lead to attitudes that favor kindness, protection, and conservation.

Trivia games have been popular recently and many of the boys may be familiar with them. Animal Pursuit is one that they can make up for themselves and play in their den meetings.

Preparation and Action

In advance, give about 25 3" x 5" cards to each boy in the den. Ask each boy to make up about 20 questions and answers. One question, with the answer on the reverse side, should be written on each card. All of the cards are to be turned in by a certain date. To avoid duplication, you may wish to assign topics — perhaps by divisions of the animal kingdom (mammals, reptiles, insects, etc.), habitat (wetlands, desert, sea, fresh water, etc.), or along some similar line. After the cards have been checked for accuracy, the game can be played using regular trivia game rules.

Reflecting

- How are animals and people alike? Do they have some of the same needs? Do they have some of the same emotions? **(O)**
- If you could trade places with an animal, what animal would you like to be? **(F)**
- Whose job should it be to take care of endangered animals? **(J)**
- What is something that you found out from playing the game today that surprised you? **(C)**

Followup

De-pet-ability. Most boys of Cub Scout and Webelos Scout age either already have one or more pets or are actively campaigning to get one. They may have the best of intentions about providing regular care, but the actual work upon which the pet's survival depends often falls to an adult. It remains true, however, that youngsters should be learning to take responsibility for their own pets.

They could use a group discussion to share information about their pets and the systems that they have worked out to make sure that they remember to provide food, water, and exercise for them. All of the ideas could be pooled into one big "de-pet-ability" system for pet care.

This could involve designing a reminder chart with checklists for daily tasks (like giving food and fresh water), as well as less frequent tasks (such as baths, shots, checkups, etc.). They might also include safety tips for protecting their animals. Once the system is in place, they could agree to make periodic reports on how it is working.

Jean Kelty's book, *If You Have a Duck . . . Adventures to Help Children Create a Humane World* (1982, George Whittell Memorial Press, 3722 South Avenue, Youngstown, Ohio 44502) contains wonderful activities to help children learn more about all kinds of animals.

More Information. There are a great many excellent films, magazines, books, and videos related to animals. Public libraries are generally wonderful resources. Commercially produced videotapes of varying length are widely available, either to rent or to borrow from a public library. Many of these videos deal with the plight of endangered species or those close to extinction. Both print and visual materials can be used to stimulate reflection and interest in finding out more.

Most states have zoos, wildlife refuges, university biology departments and schools of veterinary medicine that are good sources of information or places to visit. Less common, but also very interesting, are rehabilitation centers where injured and sick wild birds and animals are nursed back to health.

Peace Is...

This activity shows ways to introduce the positive aspects of peace, and provides suggestions for contributing to worldwide understanding.

Overview

Research done with children in the United States and in several countries of Europe has shown that although nearly all can describe war in quite graphic terms, very few can describe peace. Generally, if they come up with any definition at all, it is in such terms as: "No war," or "No bombs," or something similar. They have a very hard time thinking about peace in positive ways.

These activities use the arts to try to help the boys find new ways of thinking about peace, and about being peacemakers in their daily lives.

Preparation

The peace activities should begin with a discussion (six to eight youngsters and an adult or two make an ideal group for this). Begin with the question:

WHAT DO YOU THINK PEACE IS?

If the members of your group are typical of youngsters of Cub Scout age, they will first respond in "not war" terms. After a couple of minutes of this, gently turn the discussion (or pick up on a positive comment made by one of the boys) toward the positive aspects of peace.

Ask the group members to close their eyes for a minute and try to see something that is peaceful with their minds' eyes. Discuss their new ideas about peace. The discussion can lead into one of the following activities.

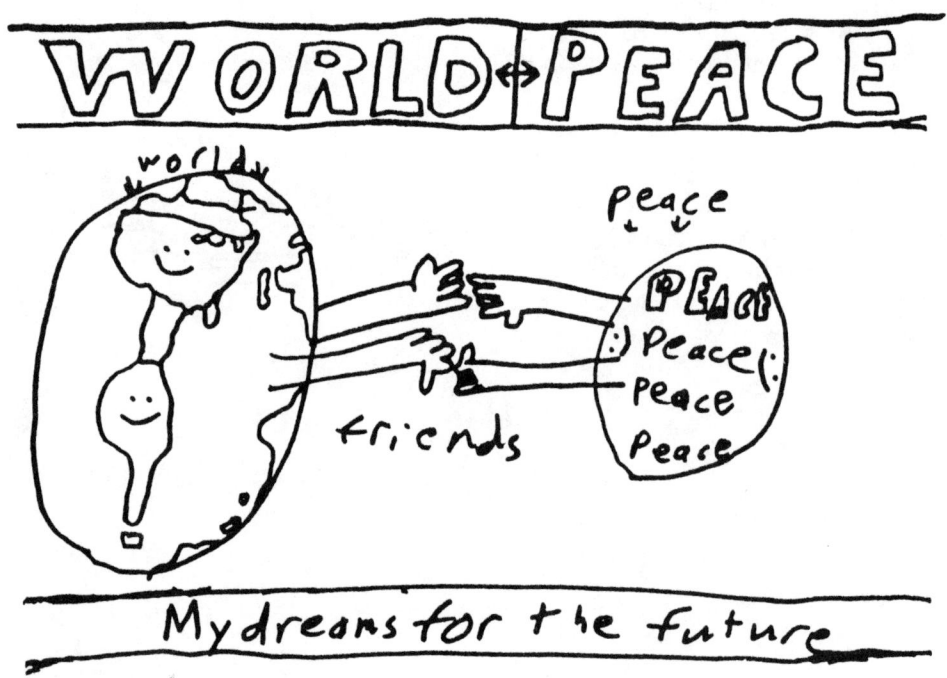

Action

COLLAGE

Even second- and third-graders may be tired of drawing because they have done it so much as part of their school work. An art technique that may be less familiar is collage. (You might want to check with the boys' schools to see if collage has been done recently in their classrooms.)

The word collage (pronounced ko-laj') comes from a French word meaning "to glue." It is a term used for artistic arrangements of various materials like paper, fabric scraps—even metal or wood, that are glued to a background surface.

Materials: A sheet of cardboard or very heavy paper, at least 9" x 12", for each boy. If you are going to use heavy materials like wood, stone, or metal in your collages, it would be best to use a sturdy material like masonite or plywood for the backing.

- White glue (If you are working with lightweight materials such as paper or feathers or fabric, you can dilute the glue to the consistency of heavy cream to make it go farther.)
- Scraps of paper (construction, tissue, wrapping papers, etc., give interesting effects); pictures from magazines, seed catalogues, etc.; scraps of fabric, wood, etc.

Making the Collage: Explain to the group what a collage is, and that a collage is made by arranging various materials in a pleasing design or picture, and then gluing the items to a backing.

Explain that they are to make a collage that will show what peace means. Some Cub Scouts will be very literal and want to glue down only cutout pictures. Try to get the boys to make a more abstract pattern that will express the feeling of peace.

The collages will take some time to dry (well beyond the time of a single meeting). The group may want to have the leader save them for a time when the boys' parents will be coming to the pack meeting. All of the peace artwork could be put on display.

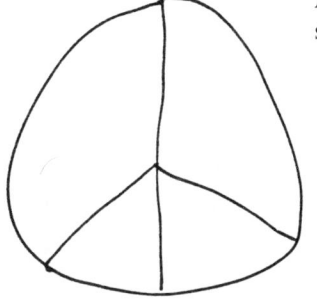

POETRY

Children as young as second-graders can write simple poems. Poetry writing activity will work best in a small group.

Materials: Pencil and paper for each boy.

Writing a Poem: You might begin by reading some poetry written by other children and suggest that the Cub Scouts try to create their own poems. The boys should be told that a poem does not need to rhyme unless the poet wants it to.

This poem was written by a sixth-grader named Bo:

MY DREAMS FOR THE FUTURE

My dreams for the future are simple,
They're what you might guess they may be,
They're basically just World Peace,
And that you would be friends with me.

I would hope that the world would be
The same as you would that they be;
All countries should love each other,
And that you would be friends with me.

And here is another by 7-year-old Kiana Fabumni (the spelling is hers):

Peace is love in our heart.
We will not fight.
We will do better things.
Me to.
We will keep the rightniss
in Gods eyes and Heart.

If some of the boys find it hard to begin, they might try to finish one of these sentences:

- Peace is like . . .
- Peace is when . . .

These are the ideas of some of the boys from one den:

- Peace is a dove
  flying in harmony above.
- Peace is giving . . .
- Peace is the silence in the sky.

Webelos Scouts may like to try a very special kind of poem called Haiku. This is a traditional form of Japanese poetry that consists of only three lines. The first line has five syllables; the second line has seven syllables, and the final line has five. In the past, Haiku was used to describe the seasons of the year, but it can be adapted to any subject.

To give you an idea of what Haiku is like, here are a couple of examples written by a boy named Jim Rapczynski when he was 12 years old.

BEST FRIENDS

We're the best of friends.
We run and play together.
We are true comrades.

GOD'S FRIEND

I am friends with God.
God provides for my spirit.
I help with his work.

Reflecting

- Do you think about peace in different ways than you did before we started to talk about it? **(O)**
- How do you think other young people in our world think about peace? Do you think that American children think about peace in ways that are different or the same as children elsewhere? **(O)**
- What are some things we can do to help make a peaceful world? **(J)**
- What feelings do you think of when we talk about peace? **(F)**
- Maybe one way to help peace to happen in the world is to have peace in ourselves and in our own families. How could we try to do this? **(C)**

Followup

Scouts may wish to copy their poems or their art and bind their work into a book. The boys could send their book to children in another country.

If one of the members of the group already has a pen-pal from another country, the group might want to send their work to this overseas friend. They could include a letter describing how the collages or poetry were produced.

A poem or drawing about peace might be made into a birthday or holiday greeting card for a special person.

At another meeting, the Cub Scouts might make peace greeting cards, and carefully copy their own poems or others that they especially like for the message on the cards.

Learn about Scouting's World Friendship Fund and make a contribution with money the group has earned.

Saying Hello, Saying Goodbye

This activity shows ways to help boys leaving or joining the pack or den and suggests ceremonies and other ways to help.

Overview

Americans are a people on the go. The average American makes 12 moves in a lifetime—three of them in childhood. Some nine million school-age children have to adapt to new homes and schools every year. One of their big worries is whether they will have friends. Research shows that, fortunately, most younger children adjust well and fairly quickly. Moving may be harder for older youngsters, however. The reasons behind a move can also make a difference in the amount of stress that children feel.

Young families are uprooted for many reasons over which children have no control. Some of these reasons are a parent's job change or promotion, or following the loss of a parent through death or divorce. Frequent moves, for whatever reason, can be very hard on children. One 12-year-old boy writing about his greatest loss, said it very poignantly:

"Home. A great loss to someone who has had to leave his family, friends, even enemies, to go live in another place many miles away ...

A new house haunts me. How different it is from my old one ... home. Home is where the heart is and the love of friends, too. Home is your tower, your castle. All smashed when the news hits of the move, just to be rebuilt at your new home ... yet a different home.

School is different, too. New teachers, names to learn, putting up with the bullies—the ones who taunt you ...

We've lived here a few months now and my tower was just being rebuilt, when SMASH—we were hit with the news—we have to move again!

My greatest loss: Home."

Even young people who move a lot work out ways of fitting in. Research tells us that groups like Cub Scout packs can be very helpful in the process of adapting to new places. Packs and dens can provide ready-made friendship groups. Cub Scouting also offers something familiar, because it is basically the same program wherever it is organized. A boy can fit in, and find a connection between his old life and his new life. The people will be new, but Cub Scouting will be the same. Cub Scouting can become what some sociologists call a "comfort zone."

However, because dens are usually formed at the beginning of the school year, boys who enter school later in the term sometimes do not get invited to join. It would be helpful if packs had plans in place for making new boys feel welcome, and for helping members who are moving away find packs to join in their new communities. (See the *Cub Scout Leader Book*, No. 3220A, for information about how to do membership transfers.)

Although most children adapt, they do react very differently to having to start over. Some boys may prevent acceptance by new groups by their own behavior. Children may recognize that they need new friends, but they may not have the social skills for getting off to a good start. Some of the ways that youngsters react to the stresses of moving are:

- Withdrawing and becoming unwilling to try to form new friendships
- Becoming so pushy in their attempts to join groups that they put people off
- Insisting that everything they left behind was a whole lot better

The new boy who is the hardest to fit into the ongoing program of the den may be the very one who needs it most. Some extra understanding on everyone's part can help.

Action

Role Play. When the members of a den learn that they are to have a new member, they might do some practicing ahead of time. Through role playing, they can develop their welcoming skills. Similar role plays could be helpful to a den member who is moving away. His old friends could help the departing Scout practice how to act when he is a new boy in a new den. Reflecting during such role plays should focus on the feelings that might be behind the way people act.

- How would you feel if you were coming into a den where you didn't know anybody? Suppose the kids laughed because the way you talked sounded different from the way they talked? **(F)**

Here are some ideas for saying hello and saying goodbye.

SAYING HELLO

Welcome Ceremony. This can also be done by a pack, with ideas contributed by the dens.

Boys of Cub Scout age enjoy rituals. Make up a special welcome ceremony for new members. It might include favorite songs, a pack yell, presentation of pack and den numerals, etc.

Welcome Book. This can be made by a single den, or dens may contribute to a pack project.

Make up a booklet of things that the boys think a new kid in town might want or need to know. The kinds of things that boys list may be quite different from what an adult would think most important. To help them get started, however, the leader might suggest:

- Cub Scouting information such as where den and pack meetings are held; where to buy Scout supplies; a short history of the den or pack; the words to special songs or yells, etc.

- The names, addresses, and phone numbers of the other boys in the den — perhaps their favorite hobbies, too.

- The best places to buy things like hobby materials, favorite kinds of food, bike supplies, etc.

- Neat places to go with their families; where the best movies are shown, etc.

SAYING GOODBYE

Losing a friend may be a sad time for members of a den or pack. Having some special ways of saying goodbye can help. The leader can help the boy find a pack to join in his new home area. The boy's membership and advancement records can go with him or can be forwarded. The local BSA council can provide information about Scouting in his new community.

Goodbye Ceremony. As with the Welcome Ceremony, this can be done by the pack or a den.

Saying goodbye will be a sentimental time. The boys should know that sad feelings are natural and that it is okay to express them openly. The ceremony that they make up should not exclude sadness, but should also allow for sharing memories of the fun they have all enjoyed together, and friends' good wishes for the future.

Memory Book. Make up a scrapbook to send with the boy who is leaving. This project might also be done as a video scrapbook if a camcorder is available. In either case, the other boys may want to do it as a surprise and show it at the goodbye ceremony before giving it to their departing friend. The boys will have a lot of ideas for what it should contain, but to help get things started, the leader might suggest:

- Pictures of den members (perhaps with a goodbye message from each) and snapshots of some of the activities that they shared

- Pictures and messages from other people (like non-Scouting friends, teachers, or neighbors)

- Pictures of town landmarks, or other places he might like to remember

Keeping in Touch. Regular notes, cards, or phone calls from his old friends, particularly for the first few months, can help a child adjust to a new place—even if he doesn't write or call back. Remembering holidays or his birthday will also provide support. If the child has not moved too far away, he might enjoy being invited back for special events.

Reflecting

- If you were moving to a new place, what would you like someone to do to help you? **(O)**

- What might it feel like to leave your friends behind? **(F)**

- Would it help us to understand a friend's feelings if we knew why he was moving? **(G)**

- What are the good things and the bad things about moving? **(J)**

- What could we do later on to show our friend that we still care about him? **(C)**

Saying No!

This activity involves making a public service announcement to help reinforce information that the boys already know about personal safety, tobacco, alcohol, drugs, etc.

Overview

Growing up has always been a serious business—particularly while one is trying to do it! Recent books, however, have referred to today's children as "endangered" (Vance Packard), "hurried" (David Elkind), and "children without childhoods" (Marie Winn). In one way or another, these writers, along with many others, are referring to the daily exposure of young people to stresses that earlier generations scarcely knew about.

Although children have been sneaking cigarettes and alcohol for as long as they have been told not to, most young people, until recently, did not have ready access to a full array of mood-altering chemicals.

Drugs are not the only ills besetting American children. As a nation, we have just begun to face up to how widespread the physical, sexual, and psychological abuse of children has become. Nationally, there are thousands of confirmed cases of abuse and neglect every year.

One way we have reacted to the plight of our children has been to develop a multitude of educational programs. These programs aim to help youngsters recognize potentially abusive situations. They provide youth with strategies for avoiding difficulties, or for seeking help when they are caught in dangerous situations.

The hope behind the design of these programs has been that children would feel empowered to prevent their own victimization. An unintended consequence, however, has been to make many young children so aware of the possibility of abuse, that they fear normal interaction with adults. Another consequence of the many prevention programs may be overexposure. Some youngsters report that they feel bombarded with information, and they are tired of hearing about it. They say they tune out when someone tries to give them more information.

At the same time, it remains true that their ignorance continues to play a part in the victimization of children. We very much want young people to be willing to say no to non-prescription drugs, alcohol, early sex, "bad touch," certain forms of peer pressure, and going with strangers. However, we have to recognize that such a ritual as "just saying no" offers no guarantee of protection. For a majority of youth, enticement does not come in the form of such a direct question as "You wanna try this?" Rather,

dangers are woven into the fabric of family, school, or neighborhood life. Children who have unmet needs or lack faith in themselves are particularly ready to accept offers of attention or recognition, regardless of who offers it. The most vulnerable of all are the growing numbers of very poor children. In 1990, for example, *one-fourth* of American boys ready to enter Tiger Cubs lived below the poverty line. The daily lives of poor children provide them with few resources and little reason to hope for a better future. Expecting these children to "just say no" without giving them positive, hope-building alternatives is irresponsible.

Having said this, we also recognize that "just say no" campaigns *do* call attention to various issues and will be familiar to most of the boys. This activity, making a public service announcement, is based on the belief that one of the best ways to reinforce learning about a subject, is to try to communicate information about it to someone else. This activity will give Cub Scouts a chance to demonstrate what they already know—and to check the accuracy of their information.

Preparation

Probably all youngsters have seen public service announcements (PSAs) during television program breaks, but they may not have distinguished them from other commercials. PSAs try to educate viewers about important issues. Stations usually do not charge the sponsor of the announcement for air time. PSAs usually vary in length from about half a minute to a minute and a half. Good ones pack a lot of impact into very little time. Since they have to stand out from regular commercials, the content of PSAs is designed to get viewers to pay attention. The leader might want to record a few public service announcements and have the boys watch them as part of the planning process. They might also want to discuss how effectively the messages came across.

For this activity, the boys will make a "Say no to . . . !" public service announcement that would be suitable for showing during one of the TV shows that a lot of youngsters watch.

The project will work best when done by a single den. However, several dens could each do a different PSA and share them at a pack meeting. Parents would no doubt enjoy seeing them.

Materials: Specific items and props needed will depend on what the boys decide to do. The activity can be done as a skit. If they want to make a permanent record of the announcement, however, a video camcorder and playback equipment will be needed. The Cub Scouts' ability to view and edit their work in progress will improve the final product. It is not easy to say much in a minute and a half. (If the boys can't fit all they want to say and do into that amount of time, they may wish to call their production a short documentary.) Multiple copies of a storyboard will be useful for planning and coordinating the script and action. A stopwatch will help with the accuracy of timing.

Action

Here are some steps to follow:

1. Choose a well-known subject. The activity will go more smoothly if the subject is one that the boys already know something about.
2. Pool information about why a young person should say no in this situation.
3. Check the accuracy of their information and seek out any additional information that is needed.
4. Decide who will be the audience for the production.
5. Plan the scenes and write the script. The storyboard will help keep the project organized.
6. Decide who will do what in the production, and get on with it.

There will be many parts to play. The most obvious are the actors, but there must also be a director, and if it is to be videotaped, a cameraman, prop-man, and so forth. The group might also want to consider using a voice over, that is, the voice of someone who is not seen on the screen. Those who have worked behind the scenes should be recognized for their efforts along with the actors. If the boys do a videotape, they could add a set of credits at the end.

Reflecting

- Can you think of times when Cub Scouts should say no? Do your friends usually come right out and ask you to do something wrong, or are there other ways that you get into bad situations together? **(O)**
- How does it feel to say no to something, especially if other kids are doing it? **(F)**
- How does it feel trying to get other people to stand up for what is right? Could this help you make a friend or could it hurt a friendship? **(J)**
- Who are some people you could trust to help you figure out what is the right thing to do? How could they help you say no to something you feel you shouldn't do? **(C)**

Followup

Other Audiences: Depending on the success of the project, the den might want to seek a wider audience. Perhaps they could show or perform their PSA for other young people and explain how and why they made it. Adult audiences such as PTAs or church groups are other possibilities.

Parents: Many parents undoubtedly will have already talked *to* their children about the subject that the Cub Scouts have chosen for the PSA. Some may not have talked *with* them about it, however. They may wish to use the activity as an opener for such a discussion.

While learning to say no is an important step in preventing self-destructive or self-defeating behavior, it is not enough. Youngsters have to have continuing reinforcement for their decisions. The best support comes from consistent, open relationships with parents and other adults and strong friendships with peers. True empowerment to say no comes from within. Children need to develop a positive self-image and along with it, a sense of efficacy—that is, the belief that they can influence what happens in their lives. Cub Scouting promotes such positive growth—particularly when there is good family and peer support.

STORY BOARD

Scene   **Plot/Notes**

Shoplifting Is Just Plain Wrong

 This activity involves a trip to see a store security system to point out the costs of shoplifting to all of us. Suggests information that boys should know about the consequences of being caught shoplifting.

Overview

Shoplifting is a major problem for American retail stores. When you add shoplifting to the related crime of theft by employees, a single suburban discount store can lose more than a quarter of a million dollars every year. As losses have climbed, stores have developed and installed more and more complicated detection systems. They are also getting tougher—even on first offenders, whatever their ages. At the same time, their out-in-the-open sales methods place items that are easy to hide where youngsters can see and handle them. This situation can be very tempting.

America is very much a consumer oriented society. Children between the ages of 4 and 12 spent more than $6 billion of their own money in 1989. Businesses now view children as independent customers and heavily advertise whole product lines that were created just for young people. It is very easy for youngsters to think that they must have "in" things to be successful and popular among peers. It is not really surprising that young children try out shoplifting as a way of getting things that they "need," or badly want. However, for whatever reason it is done, shoplifting is just plain wrong! Shoplifting is a crime.

Children begin to shoplift at about age 6 or 7. This is about the age that many parents begin to allow children to go to toy departments on their own. At this age, boys tend to be much more bold in their actions. They go for it! The items they pick out to steal are candy, small popular toys, water pistols, and so forth. For this age, the typical "M-O" (that is, modus operandi, or way of doing it) is to remove an item from the shelf, take it out of the package to see how it works, play with it a bit, decide it is wanted, and put it into a pocket. Often, parents have no idea that a crime has taken place.

Den leaders may wish to share with the boys' parents these rules that security officers feel can help prevent early offenses:

1. Do not permit young children to wander alone in "zones of temptation" such as toy or candy departments. If no adult supervision is available, they should be with a trusted older sibling or friend.

2. Do not permit children to open any package until after the item has been paid for. Packaged goods are more difficult to conceal. If children really need to look at an item before they can decide whether or not to buy it, most stores will permit the customer to look at the item under the supervision of a store employee.

3. Parents should be prepared to cooperate with the store in the event that a child is found to have something that does not belong to him and that has not been paid for. Store policies and state and local laws on arresting shoplifters vary according to the age of the culprit and the size of the crime. It is hard not to be embarrassed when one's child is caught. In the long run, it is more important that the child is impressed with the seriousness of what he or she has done.

Young children are not particularly clever at hiding things. Some first offenders may be naive enough to take out the stolen item and play with it while on the way home. According to store security officials, the most effective way of handling the situation when a stolen item is discovered is to go back to the store. There, the child must be made to confess to the security officer, and the item must be paid for.

They suggest that the child be made to pay for the item with his own funds. If he does not have enough on hand, an advance from his parents may be necessary. If so, a plan should be made for repaying his parents from future earnings or allowance. Few stores keep records on first offenders under 8 years of age. However, they may ask that in the future, a family member keep the youngster under close supervision whenever he is in the store.

Children 8 and over tend to be more skilled at concealing stolen items, both at the time of the theft and after they get them home. Their tastes are more sophisticated as well.

Older children are more likely to steal video movies, cassette tapes, sports equipment, jewelry, novelty items, and popular items of clothing. Given the normal borrowing patterns of early adolescents, it is not always easy for a parent to figure out the source of some items found among a child's things. Parents should be alert to the possibility that an item has been stolen, and be prepared to do some checking and take appropriate action.

Store security employees are trained to do some checking of their own. Any time an item is concealed, a security officer may legally detain a suspect. Some stores, however, wait to give people every opportunity to pay for the item in question, and do not stop a suspect until he or she goes through the door.

Generally, the law becomes harder on youngsters over 8. While a store can make up its own policies toward younger children, in many states, the law holds 8-year-olds responsible. Most stores will carry out the law. The store must call the police and file a report on any incident—even a first offense. A contact card is started for the child, and a court appearance before a judge may be necessary. Many communities are developing special programs for young offenders that may involve fines, work, or community service. Repeat offenders risk being locked up.

Fear of punishment may prevent 6- and 7-year-olds from shoplifting. This is particularly true if they have been caught on their first tries, and if justice has been served swiftly and fairly. Older youngsters may not be daunted as easily. These young people may believe that they are clever enough not to get caught (as, in truth, some may be). However, boys of this age are ready to see that breaking the law by shoplifting has consequences for themselves, and for their communities. Some of these are:

- They will not feel good about themselves, knowing that they have broken the law. They may live with the fear that someone will find out—not a good way to feel.

- Once people find out that they have stolen something, it may be hard to gain back the trust that was lost.

- Parents may not trust them and let them go places that they want to go.

- Friends and other young people may not trust them around their property.

- The store may not let them come back again.

- Shoplifting costs the store real money. A general estimate is that when one item is stolen, the store has to sell 100 items like it to make up for the loss. This means that the store has to raise prices to cover the money it loses from shoplifting. It also costs the store money to pay for the security systems that are necessary to cut down on theft. It costs the community money to carry out the laws in the courts and the juvenile detention facilities. All of these costs mean higher prices and higher taxes.

In the discussion that follows the activity, any of these points that the boys do not bring up by themselves might be noted by the leader.

Preparation

This activity involves a field trip to a store large enough to have a system of security that will be interesting to the boys. Most stores will be open to having Cub Scouts and Webelos Scouts come in for this purpose, but careful advance preparation is necessary. A good field trip of this sort should last about half an hour—longer if there is much to see and interest remains high.

Call the store well in advance to make arrangements. Ask about such details as:

1. How many boys can come at one time? (Perhaps two dens could go together if the store can handle a group of that size.)
2. Explain to the store personnel what you hope to get from the trip. Ask about what the boys will be able to see (e.g., one-way mirrors, alarms, floor-walkers and security officers, hand-cuffs, etc.).
3. Ask that the store be ready to explain just what happens to youngsters who are caught for the first time, and for repeat offenses.

After the details of time, place, and content are arranged, confirm them in writing.

Prepare the Cub Scouts by discussing the problems of shoplifting in advance of the field trip to the store. Explain some of the things that they may expect to see, and spell out how you expect them to behave while they are in the store.

Action

Be on time and keep to the schedule agreed upon with the store.

Reinforce what has been presented by the store. Encourage the boys to ask questions. Try to clear up any misunderstandings that they may have. Leaders should also be sensitive to the possibility that one or more of the boys may have already tried out shoplifting. Leaders should be prepared to help such youngsters deal with the anxiety that may arise from the field trip.

Reflecting

- What do you think about shoplifting? **(O)**
- How do you suppose someone might feel after taking something from a store without paying for it? Would that feeling go away? **(F)**
- How would you feel toward someone if you knew he or she had shoplifted? How could you help that person at another time? **(J)**
- What are some of the things that happen in a store when people shoplift? **(G)**
- From what we have talked about and seen at the store, are there things that we can do to help with this problem? **(C)**

Followup

Store personnel always appreciate thank-you notes from youngsters. If each boy included a comment or two about what he had learned, further reinforcement would be provided.

Most parents welcome help from the Cub Scouts in reinforcing what they are teaching at home about honesty and trustworthiness. Parents may wish to continue the discussion about what the youngster has learned, when he gets home.

What We Say

This activity deals with name-calling and tattling that are typical Cub Scout age behaviors, but nevertheless are actions that can be very disruptive and painful. Because most of the activities are short and require no materials or advance preparation, they can be used when a need arises.

Overview

Sticks and stones
Can break my bones,
But names can never hurt me!

But names can hurt, as anyone who has yelled these lines back after an insult knows. The words children use can sometimes be very upsetting, both to adults and to other children.

The Cub Scout years have been described by one psychologist as the time when nice children begin to behave in most awful ways. Psychologist Gesell and his associates followed a group of children from birth through adolescence. These researchers noticed that there were two periods in the lives of the children that were characterized by what they called "verbal violence." These periods were at about the ages of 6 and 11.

Such a finding is not too surprising, for these years are about the same times when children are entering more complicated phases of mental and moral development. Although it may not be particularly comforting, it is nonetheless true that some of their verbal hostility is a reflection of some new mental skills.

Six-year-olds are beginning to understand that other people have motivations for their behavior. Youngsters also realize that they can provoke certain kinds of response from others. While "You scratch my back, I'll scratch yours" is foremost in their approach to moral reasoning, around age 6 is also a time when children use others' actions as excuses for their own verbal misdeeds—as in the many variations on the theme of: "He did it to me first!" or "He made me do it!"

Eleven-year-olds are not only getting more accurate in the ways that they see themselves, but are developing skill in imagining how they are seen by other people. At this age, youngsters are getting better at putting themselves in the place of others. These new abilities are necessary for a

full understanding of the golden rule, which is "Do unto others *as you would have them do unto you.*" Boys who have reached this point in their development begin to understand what really matters to another person. When used positively, these "mutual role-taking skills" can be the foundation for more caring, mature friendships and relationships with family members. The same skills, however, enable boys of this age to zero in on others' sensitive points and strike where it hurts most.

The fact that verbal violence may be considered developmentally normal doesn't change the fact that it may also have harmful effects. Studies have confirmed what anyone who works with youth already knows: children who ridicule, blame, and threaten others are not popular with their peers. On the other hand, children who pay attention to others, praise them, and show an appropriate amount of affection towards them are well liked.

Name-calling in its extreme form becomes bullying and may be accompanied by other forms of aggression. Researchers have followed young bullies into adulthood. These studies showed that childhood bullies did not outgrow their behavior without help. If left unchecked, many childhood bullies became aggressive, and often abusive adults. Many of the victims of bullies also bore scars, such as not liking themselves, into adulthood.

Because there are damaging outcomes to verbal violence, there are good reasons for stopping behaviors such as name-calling and tattling when they show up among Cub Scouts.

The reasons why children use such verbal behavior vary. We have already noted that one reason may be simply because they have discovered that they can do it, and that it brings results. Normal children are looking for ways to bring about control over their lives. Much of children's behavior is experimental. If an action works, it is likely to be repeated; if not, it is usually dropped. There are children, however, whose normal needs for recognition and control are not being met. Such youngsters may keep acting in ways that bring attention, even though that attention is negative.

Preparation

Some form of verbal violence such as name-calling, tattling, or tale-bearing is bound to occur in the den or pack setting. These are some of the things that nearly all boys of Cub Scout age do! Just making rules outlawing such behavior is not likely to have much effect in the long run. However, getting the boys to agree that such behavior is not acceptable at den meetings is a place to start. "Verbal violence" is best dealt with *when it occurs*. In working through a persistent problem the leader will have to be sensitive to whether the trouble is between two boys, or more widespread in the group. In either case, discussion of feelings can help bring the situation out into the open. These games can help get the conversation started.

Action

GOOD SCOUTS . . .

This activity can be used to open a meeting, and can be repeated often, if the boys enjoy it. Have the boys sit in a circle. Each one says something good about the person on his left. After they have gone all the way around, go around again the other way.

IT MAKES ME FEEL _____ WHEN . . .

This game can be used to start a discussion about feelings. Before the meeting when the game is to be played, the leader writes words that describe feelings such as happy, sad, angry, etc., on cards, or boys could prepare the cards.

To play the game, have the Cub Scouts sit in a circle. One draws a card, and the word written on the card is used to fill in the blank in the sentence: "It makes me feel _____ when . . ." Each boy, in turn, names something that makes him feel that way, too. One or several cards can be used at a meeting.

CONSEQUENCES

Den members can make up their own consequence rule that is called into play when verbal violence occurs.

Reflecting

- How does it feel to talk about feelings? **(F)**

- Is it hard or easy to talk about feelings? Is it good to let other people know how you feel? What can happen if you share feelings? **(J)**

- If people around you don't know how you feel, sometimes they guess. Do you think that they usually guess right or wrong? **(G)**

- Is it worth it to tell another person how you are really feeling? **(C)**

Action

GOSSIP

Just about everyone at some time in his or her life learns firsthand about the embarrassment and unfairness involved when one is a victim of a story that is not true. Gossip is a very old game that has been played by many generations of American young people. The game of Gossip demonstrates how hard it is to keep things straight when details get passed on by word of mouth.

Members of the group sit in a semicircle. Player 1 (who is sitting at one end) starts a message by whispering it to player 2, who, in turn, whispers it to player 3, and so on, down the line. When the gossip has gone all the way to the end, the last player to receive the message tells the group what he heard. Then, player 1 tells the group the original message. They are rarely the same—sometimes they are not even close!

Good messages for Gossip involve names, numbers, and other details. Here are some samples:

- Jason saw six kids run out of the store carrying stuff in eight bags.
- Five kids had to stay after school because they talked too loud in class.
- Have you heard? There might be a storm with lots of wind and rain and maybe some hail and a tornado.

Reflecting

In real life, too, messages can get completely changed as gossip passes from one person to another. Sometimes a youngster's reputation can be hurt in the process. The boys will no doubt have examples to tell about from their own experiences.

- Have you ever had a mixed-up message given to you? What happened? **(O)**
- Could someone get hurt or get into trouble because of a mixed-up message? **(J)**
- Do you agree or disagree with this statement: Some gossip isn't worth passing on—even if it is true—if it might hurt someone's reputation. **(J)**
- How does it feel to have other people talk about you behind your back? **(F)**
- If someone you know is in trouble and needs help, is it "gossip" to tell a person who can give that help? **(C)**

When Bad Things Happen

This is not an activity for Cub Scouts, but provides ideas for leaders to help them promote understanding of a special problem of an individual Scout, or of the group as a whole.

Overview

No matter how hard we try to protect children, they can run up against some of life's harsh realities. Some things happen all at once, such as a serious accident or illness; a divorce; or the death of a parent, grandparent, sibling, friend, or even of a much-loved pet. Other things can go on for a long time in the life of a child. Some of these problems include chronic illness, physical or sexual abuse, or the chemical dependency of someone close. How a youngster is helped to handle a problem at the time that it occurs is a determining factor in how badly the child will be hurt.

There really are no ways for a Cub Scout leader to prepare for such troubles. A leader can, however, be sensitive and learn to be a very good listener, and try to be aware of what may be happening in the lives of the boys. An upset child is more likely to confide in an adult whom he trusts and with whom he already feels safe.

Without adult help, young boys may have difficulty in being the kinds of friends that are needed by a child with a serious problem. In fact, by reacting to behavior that they do not understand, youngsters may even add to a troubled child's distress. With some guidance, however, Cub Scouts can be encouraged and enabled to become a true support group for children with special needs.

Today's children are remarkably aware of what is happening to other children, but they may have little understanding of how and why such things happen. Not discussing problems does not make worries go away.

Reactions to Problems. When something tragic happens to another child, particularly one whom they know, boys of Cub Scout and Webelos Scout age typically wonder, "Will the same thing happen to me?"

While adults may understand that the odds are against it, young children do not. Youngsters need reassurance, but at this age take promises very literally. Their ideas of cause and effect are often incomplete, or simply wrong. The same is true of children's sense of what they can and cannot control in their lives.

Another typical reaction to tragedy among children of Cub Scout or Webelos Scout age is: "It's my fault!"

They think: "If I'd been nicer, smarter, better, had done as I was told, or something, it would not have happened." This response is often found when parents divorce, or when something happens to a sibling with whom a child has had a normal amount of rivalry. Adults can offer assurance to a youngster that it was not something he or she did or did not do that brought on the predicament.

Children can also be helped to develop some coping skills. They also gain a sense of empowerment through helping others deal with problems. An understanding Cub Scout leader and a supportive group of friends can go a long way toward easing a child's burden. But problems are sometimes of such enormity that children require professional help.

Family Problems. When researchers ask young children about their worries, high on their lists is fear that a parent will die—fortunately not a reality for most youngsters. However, also high on lists of children's worries is fear that their parents will divorce. Such a fear is not unfounded, for divorce is likely to be a reality in the lives of about half of young Americans before their 18th birthdays. Children need a great deal of reassurance that they will always have the love of both of their parents. Unfortunately, comfort isn't always there, and a youngster may act out his distress in ways that are disruptive and make other children (and adults) angry.

Illness. Youngsters may shun another child who has a life-threatening disease such as cancer, because they fear it is contagious. Adults should provide accurate information about the disease and allow young people to discuss their questions and fears openly. If the sick child is someone whom the boys know, they should also be told something about what he or she is going through as part of the treatment process.

Sick children need understanding friends in very special ways. Sometimes treatment or medication causes changes in appearance or behavior as side-effects. Their friends can be helped to understand such side-effects and to take them into account. If the child is hospitalized, friends can do special things to let him or her know that they care. The boys will undoubtedly come up with some very good ideas about ways they can help and show compassion during a friend's hard times.

Abuse. The abuse and neglect of children and adolescents know no ethnic or socioeconomic boundaries. We have been appalled to find the extent to which American children are suffering at the hands of adults. Suspected abuse and/or neglect must be reported or brought to the attention of someone (a physician, school counselor, nurse, or principal, etc.) required by law to report it. Most frequently (about 75 percent of the time) the abuser is someone whom the child knows—a parent or grandparent, older sibling or other relative, or a neighbor or family friend—not a stranger, as popular opinion may suggest. To date, the abuse of young females has received more attention, but boys are also frequent victims.

We do not know as much about the extent of victimization of young males, partly because boys are even less likely than girls to report abuse. The BSA offers youth protection training to professional staff and volunteers in all levels of the program.

Preparation

INVOLVING PARENTS

The 1980s saw rapid change in American families. More children were being raised in homes where there was only one parent. One in five children under the age of 18 lived in a family with income that fell below the poverty line (the figure was one in four for children under the age of 6). Women with young children entered the labor force in unprecedented numbers. For most families with two wage-earners, two incomes were required to furnish necessities—not luxuries. Many adults caring for their children are also caring for aging parents. In fact, the old ideal of the family—a working father, a stay-at-home mother, and their children—now applies to fewer than one in 10 American households. All of these changes have added to family stress levels, and do make it more diffult for many parents to get involved in their son's Cub Scout and Webelos Scout activities. However, experience suggests that leaders who, from the outset, expect parents to be involved are more likely to gain their interest and support.

Most parents will want to know about a problem being faced by one of their son's friends, or of difficulties occuring in the den. They may wish to be present at the meeting when the dicussion of the problem takes place. Or they may wish to follow up with further discussion at home.

While one might like to believe that all parents would appreciate a Cub Scout leader bringing a child's distress to their attention, this is not always the case—particularly if a parent is the source of the problem. Sometimes help from school counselors or clergy can be enlisted. This approach would be especially appropriate when a school or religious body is the chartered organization for the pack.

Special information and help may be needed to enable the den or pack to deal with a problem. Sometimes expertise can be found among the parents of the pack members or through the chartered organization. If starting out cold, a good source of information in most communities is the local United Way's help line number.

Action

There is no formula for dealing with the serious problems that may confront young Cub Scouts. The best approach is open, honest, informed, and sensitive discussion of the specific situation. Some leaders have found reading children's stories aloud an effective way to introduce difficult subjects to the den.

Reflecting

The process of reflecting—using discussion to help make sense of things—is also appropriate when helping boys deal with problems, even though the boys may not have shared the same experience. Questions can also be used to open up discussion of ways to be helpful.

- When something bad happens, is it better to talk about it or keep it to yourself? What makes you think that? **(J)**

- If you think someone is feeling bad, is it okay to ask if you can help? **(F)**

- Sometimes just listening to someone with a problem can make that person feel better. What are some ways to be a good listener? **(G)**

- If a friend talks to you about a big problem, is it okay to tell an adult who might be able to help? Should you first tell your friend what you are going to do? **(C)**